In Defense of Anarchism

*the text of this book is printed
on 100% recycled paper*

HARPER ESSAYS IN PHILOSOPHY

Edited by Arthur C. Danto

Arthur C. Danto — What Philosophy Is
Jerrold J. Katz — The Underlying Reality of Language and Its Philosophical Import
Norman Malcolm — Problems of Mind
David Pears — What Is Knowledge?
Bernard Williams — Morality: An Introduction to Ethics
Robert Paull Wolff — In Defense of Anarchism
Richard Wollheim — Art and Its Objects

In Defense of Anarchism

Robert Paul Wolff

HARPER COLOPHON BOOKS
Harper & Row, Publishers
New York, Hagerstown, San Francisco, London

First HARPER TORCHBOOK edition published 1970

LIBRARY OF CONGRESS CATALOG CARD NUMBER: 78-121839
   77 78 79 80 13 12 10

Contents

— ◆ ▬◆▬ ◆ —

Preface

————◆•◆————

This essay on the foundations of the authority of the state marks a stage in the development of my concern with problems of political authority and moral autonomy. When I first became deeply interested in the subject, I was quite confident that I could find a satisfactory justification for the traditional democratic doctrine to which I rather unthinkingly gave my allegiance. Indeed, during my first year as a member of the Columbia University Philosophy Department, I taught a course on political philosophy in which I boldly announced that I would formulate and then solve the fundamental problem of political philosophy. I had no trouble formulating the problem—roughly speaking, how the moral autonomy of the individual can be made compatible with the legitimate authority of the state. I also had no trouble refuting a number of supposed solutions which had been put forward by various theorists of the democratic state. But midway through the semester, I was forced to go before my class, crestfallen and very embarrassed, to announce that I had failed to discover the grand solution.

At first, as I struggled with this dilemma, I clung to the conviction that a solution lay just around the next conceptual corner. When I read papers on the subject to meetings at various universities, I was forced again and again to represent myself as searching for a theory which I simply could not find. Little by little, I began to shift the emphasis of my exposition. Finally—whether from philosophical reflection, or simply from chagrin—I came to the realization that I was really defending the negative rather than looking for the positive. My failure to find any theoretical justification for the authority of the state had convinced me that there was no justification. In short, I had become a philosophical anarchist.

The first chapter of this essay formulates the problem as I originally posed it to myself more than five years ago. The second chapter explores the classical democratic solution to the problem and exposes the inadequacy of the usual majoritarian model of the democratic state. The third chapter sketches, in a rather impressionistic, Hegelian way, the reasons for my lingering hope that a solution can be found; it concludes with some brief, quite utopian suggestions of ways in which an anarchic society might actually function.

Leaving aside any flaws which may lurk in the arguments actually presented in these pages, this essay suffers from two major inadequacies. On the side of pure theory, I have been forced to *assume* a number of very important propositions about the nature, sources, and limits of moral obligation. To put it bluntly, I have simply taken for granted an entire ethical theory. On the side of practical application, I have said almost nothing about the material, social, or psychological conditions under which anarchism might be a feasible mode of social organization. I am painfully aware of these defects, and it is my hope to publish a full-scale work in the reasonably near future in which a great deal more will be said on both subjects. If I may steal a title from Kant (and thus perhaps wrap myself in the cloak of his legitimacy), this essay might rather grandly be subtitled *Groundwork of the Metaphysics of the State.*

New York City, March, 1970

In Defense of Anarchism

I.
The Conflict Between Authority and Autonomy

———◆◆◆———

1. The Concept of Authority

Politics is the exercise of the power of the state, or the attempt to influence that exercise. Political philosophy is therefore, strictly speaking, the philosophy of the state. If we are to determine the content of political philosophy, and whether indeed it exists, we must begin with the concept of the state.

The state is a group of persons who have and exercise supreme authority within a given territory. Strictly, we should say that a state is a group of persons who have supreme authority within a given territory *or over a certain population*. A nomadic tribe may exhibit the authority structure of a state, so long as its subjects do not fall under the superior authority of a territorial state.[1] The state may

1. For a similar definition of "state," see Max Weber, *Politics as a Vocation.* Weber emphasizes the means—force—by which the will of the state is imposed, but a careful analysis of his definition shows

include all the persons who fall under its authority, as does the democratic state according to its theorists; it may also consist of a single individual to whom all the rest are subject. We may doubt whether the one-person state has ever actually existed, although Louis XIV evidently thought so when he announced, "L'état, c'est moi." The distinctive characteristic of the state is supreme authority, or what political philosophers used to call "sovereignty." Thus one speaks of "popular sovereignty," which is the doctrine that the people are the state, and of course the use of "sovereign" to mean "king" reflects the supposed concentration of supreme authority in a monarchy.

Authority is the right to command, and correlatively, the right to be obeyed. It must be distinguished from power, which is the ability to compel compliance, either through the use or the threat of force. When I turn over my wallet to a thief who is holding me at gunpoint, I do so because the fate with which he threatens me is worse than the loss of money which I am made to suffer. I grant that he has power over me, but I would hardly suppose that he has *authority*, that is, that he has a right to demand my money and that I have an obligation to give it to him. When the government presents me with a bill for taxes, on the other hand, I pay it (normally) even though I do not wish to, and even if I think I can get away with not paying. It is, after all, the duly constituted government, and hence it has a *right* to tax me. It has *authority* over me. Sometimes, of course, I cheat the government, but even so, I acknowledge its authority, for who would speak of "cheating" a thief?

---

that it also bases itself on the notion of authority ("imperative coordination").

To *claim* authority is to claim the right to be obeyed. To *have* authority is then—what? It may mean to have that right, or it may mean to have one's claim acknowledged and accepted by those at whom it is directed. The term "authority" is ambiguous, having both a descriptive and a normative sense. Even the descriptive sense refers to norms or obligations, of course, but it does so by *describing* what men believe they ought to do rather than by *asserting* that they ought to do it.

Corresponding to the two senses of authority, there are two concepts of the state. Descriptively, the state may be defined as a group of persons who are *acknowledged* to have supreme authority within a territory—acknowledged, that is, by those over whom the authority is asserted. The study of the forms, characteristics, institutions, and functioning of *de facto* states, as we may call them, is the province of political science. If we take the term in its prescriptive signification, the state is a group of persons who have the *right* to exercise supreme authority within a territory. The discovery, analysis, and demonstration of the forms and principles of legitimate authority—of the right to rule—is called political philosophy.

What is meant by *supreme* authority? Some political philosophers, speaking of authority in the normative sense, have held that the true state has ultimate authority over all matters whatsoever that occur within its venue. Jean-Jacques Rousseau, for example, asserted that the social contract by which a just political community is formed "gives to the body politic absolute command over the members of which it is formed; and it is this power, when directed by the general will, that bears . . . the name of 'sovereignty.'" John Locke, on the other hand, held that the supreme authority of the just state extends only to those matters which it is proper for a state to control. The state is, to be sure, the highest authority, but its right to command is less than absolute. One of the questions which political philosophy must answer is whether there is any limit to the range of affairs over which a just state has authority.

An authoritative command must also be distinguished from a persuasive argument. When I am commanded to do something, I may choose to comply even though I am not being threatened, because I am brought to believe that it is something which I ought to do. If that is the case, then I am not, strictly speaking, obeying a command, but rather acknowledging the force of an argument or the rightness of a prescription. The person who issues the "command" functions merely as the *occasion* for my becoming aware of my duty, and his role might in other instances be filled by an admonishing friend, or even by my own conscience. I might, by an extension of the term, say that the prescription has authority over me, meaning simply that I ought to act in accordance with it. But the person himself has no authority—or, to be more precise, my complying with his command does not constitute an acknowledgment on my part of any such authority. Thus authority resides in persons; they possess it—if indeed they do at all—by virtue of who they are and not by virtue of what they command. My duty to obey is a duty owed to them, not to the moral law or to the beneficiaries of the actions I may be commanded to perform.

There are, of course, many reasons why men actually acknowledge claims of authority. The most common, taking the whole of human history, is simply the prescriptive force of tradition. The fact that something has always been done in a certain way strikes most men as a perfectly adequate reason for doing it that way again. Why should we submit to a king? Because we have always submitted to kings. But why should the oldest son of the king become king in turn? Because oldest sons have always been heirs to the throne. The force of the traditional is engraved so deeply on men's minds that even a study of the violent and haphazard origins of a ruling family will not weaken its authority in the eyes of its subjects.

Some men acquire the aura of authority by virtue of their own extraordinary characteristics, either as great military leaders, as men of saintly character, or as forceful personalities. Such men gather followers and disciples around them who willingly obey without consideration of personal interest or even against its dictates. The followers believe that the leader has a *right to command,* which is to say, *authority.*

Most commonly today, in a world of bureaucratic armies and institutionalized religions, when kings are few in number and the line of prophets has run out, authority is granted to those who occupy official positions. As Weber has pointed out, these positions appear authoritative in the minds of most men because they are defined by certain sorts of bureaucratic regulations having the virtues of publicity, generality, predictability, and so forth. We become conditioned to respond to the visible signs of officiality, such as printed forms and badges. Sometimes we may have clearly in mind the justification for a legalistic claim to authority, as when we comply with a command because its author is an *elected* official. More often the mere sight of a uniform is enough to make us feel that the man inside it has a right to be obeyed.

That men accede to claims of supreme authority is plain.
That men *ought* to accede to claims of supreme authority
is not so obvious. Our first question must therefore be,
Under what conditions and for what reasons does one man
have supreme authority over another? The same question
can be restated, Under what conditions can a state (under-
stood normatively) exist?

Kant has given us a convenient title for this sort of investigation. He called it a "deduction," meaning by the
term not a proof of one proposition from another, but a
demonstration of the legitimacy of a concept. When a concept is empirical, its deduction is accomplished merely by
pointing to instances of its objects. For example, the deduction of the concept of a horse consists in exhibiting a
horse. Since there are horses, it must be legitimate to em-
ploy the concept. Similarly, a deduction of the descriptive
concept of a state consists simply in pointing to the in-
numerable examples of human communities in which some
men claim supreme authority over the rest and are obeyed.
But when the concept in question is nonempirical, its deduction must proceed in a different manner. All normative
concepts are nonempirical, for they refer to what ought to
be rather than to what is. Hence, we cannot justify the use
of the concept of (normative) supreme authority by pre-
senting instances.[2] We must demonstrate by an *a priori*
argument that there can be forms of human community in
which some men have a moral right to rule. In short, the
fundamental task of political philosophy is to provide a
deduction of the concept of the state.

2. For each time we offered an example of legitimate authority,
we would have to attach to it a nonempirical argument proving the
legitimacy.

To complete this deduction, it is not enough to show that there are circumstances in which men have an obligation to do what the *de facto* authorities command. Even under the most unjust of governments there are frequently good reasons for obedience rather than defiance. It may be that the government has commanded its subjects to do what in fact they already have an independent obligation to do; or it may be that the evil consequences of defiance far outweigh the indignity of submission. A government's commands may promise beneficent effects, either intentionally or not. For these reasons, and for reasons of prudence as well, a man may be right to comply with the commands of the government under whose *de facto* authority he finds himself. But none of this settles the question of legitimate authority. That is a matter of the *right* to command, and of the correlative obligation *to obey the person who issues the command.*

The point of the last paragraph cannot be too strongly stressed. Obedience is not a matter of doing what someone tells you to do. It is a matter of doing what he tells you to do *because he tells you to do it.* Legitimate, or *de jure,* authority thus concerns the grounds and sources of moral obligation.

Since it is indisputable that there are men who believe that others have authority over them, it might be thought that we could use that fact to prove that somewhere, at some time or other, there must have been men who really did possess legitimate authority. We might think, that is to say, that although some claims to authority might be wrong, it could not be that *all* such claims were wrong, since then we never would have had the concept of legitimate authority at all. By a similar argument, some philosophers have tried to show that not all our experiences are dreams, or more generally that in experience not everything is mere apearance rather than reality. The point is that terms like "dream" and "appearance" are defined by contrast with "waking experience" or "reality." Hence we could only have developed a use for them by being presented with situations in which some experiences were dreams and others not, or some things mere appearance and others reality.

Whatever the force of that argument in general, it cannot be applied to the case of *de facto* versus *de jure* authority, for the key component of both concepts, namely "right," is imported into the discussion from the realm of moral philosophy generally. Insofar as we concern ourselves with the possibility of a just state, we *assume* that moral discourse is meaningful and that adequate deductions have been given of concepts like "right," "duty," and "obligation."[3]

What can be inferred from the existence of *de facto* states is that men *believe* in the existence of legitimate authority, for of course a *de facto* state is simply a state whose subjects believe it to be legitimate (i.e., really to have the authority which it claims for itself). They may be wrong. Indeed, *all* beliefs in authority may be wrong—there may be not a single state in the history of mankind which has now or ever has had a right to be obeyed. It might even be impossible for such a state to exist; that is the question we must try to settle. But so long as men believe in the au-

3. Thus, political philosophy is a dependent or derivative discipline, just as the philosophy of science is dependent upon the general theory of knowledge and on the branches of metaphysics which concern themselves with the reality and nature of the physical world.

thority of states, we can conclude that they possess the concept of *de jure* authority.[4]

The normative concept of the state as the human community which possesses rightful authority within a territory thus defines the subject matter of political philosophy proper. However, even if it should prove impossible to present a deduction of the concept—if, that is, there can be no *de jure* state—still a large number of moral questions can be raised concerning the individual's relationship with *de facto* states. We may ask, for example, whether there are any moral principles which ought to guide the state in its lawmaking, such as the principle of utilitarianism, and under what conditions it is right for the individual to obey the laws. We may explore the social ideals of equality and achievement, or the principles of punishment, or the justifications for war. All such investigations are essentially applications of general moral principles to the particular phenomena of (*de facto*) politics. Hence, it would be appropriate to reclaim a word which has fallen on bad days, and call that branch of the study of politics *casuistical politics*. Since there are men who acknowledge claims to authority, there are *de facto* states. Assuming that moral discourse in general is legitimate, there must be moral questions which arise in regard to such states. Hence, casuistical politics as a branch of ethics does exist. It re-

---

4. This point is so simple that it may seem unworthy of such emphasis. Nevertheless, a number of political philosophers, including Hobbes and John Austin, have supposed that *the concept* as well as the principles of authority could be derived from the concepts of power or utility. For example, Austin defines a command as a signification of desire, uttered by someone who will visit evil on those who do not comply with it (*The Providence of Jurisprudence Determined*, Lecture I).

mains to be decided whether political philosophy proper exists.

2. The Concept of Autonomy

The fundamental assumption of moral philosophy is that men are responsible for their actions. From this assumption it follows necessarily, as Kant pointed out, that men are metaphysically free, which is to say that in some sense they are capable of choosing how they shall act. Being able to choose how he acts makes a man responsible, but merely choosing is not in itself enough to constitute *taking* responsibility for one's actions. Taking responsibility involves attempting to determine what one ought to do, and that, as philosophers since Aristotle have recognized, lays upon one the additional burdens of gaining knowledge, reflecting on motives, predicting outcomes, criticizing principles, and so forth.

The obligation to take responsibility for one's actions does not derive from man's freedom of will alone, for more is required in taking responsibility than freedom of choice. Only because man has the capacity to reason about his choices can he be said to stand under a continuing obligation to take responsibility for them. It is quite appropriate that moral philosophers should group together children and madmen as beings not fully responsible for their actions, for as madmen are thought to lack freedom of choice, so children do not yet possess the power of reason in a developed form. It is even just that we should assign a greater degree of responsibility to children, for madmen, by virtue of their lack of free will, are completely without responsibility, while children, insofar as they possess reason in a partially developed form, can be held responsible (i.e., can be required to take responsibility) to a corresponding degree.

Every man who possesses both free will and reason has an obligation to take responsibility for his actions, even though he may not be actively engaged in a continuing process of reflection, investigation, and deliberation about how he ought to act. A man will sometimes announce his willingness to take responsibility for the consequences of his actions, even though he has not deliberated about them, or does not intend to do so in the future. Such a declaration is, of course, an advance over the refusal to take responsibility; it at least acknowledges the existence of the obligation. But it does not relieve the man of the duty to engage in the reflective process which he has thus far shunned. It goes without saying that a man may take responsibility for his actions and yet act wrongly. When we describe someone as a responsible individual, we do not imply that he always does what is right, but only that he does not neglect the duty of attempting to ascertain what is right.

The responsible man is not capricious or anarchic, for he does acknowledge himself bound by moral constraints. But he insists that he alone is the judge of those constraints. He may listen to the advice of others, but he makes it his own by determining for himself whether it is good advice. He may learn from others about his moral obligations, but only in the sense that a mathematician learns from other mathematicians—namely by hearing from them arguments whose validity he recognizes even though he did not think of them himself. He does not learn in the sense that one learns from an explorer, by accepting as true his accounts of things one cannot see for oneself.

Since the responsible man arrives at moral decisions

which he expresses to himself in the form of impera-
tives, we may say that he gives laws to himself, or is self-
legislating. In short, he is *autonomous*. As Kant argued,
moral autonomy is a combination of freedom and responsibility; it is a submission to laws which one has made for
oneself. The autonomous man, insofar as he is autonomous,
is not subject to the will of another. He may do what another tells him, but not *because* he has been told to do it.
He is therefore, in the political sense of the word, *free*.

Since man's responsibility for his actions is a conse-
quence of his capacity for choice, he cannot give it up or
put it aside. He can refuse to acknowledge it, however,
either deliberately or by simply failing to recognize his
moral condition. All men refuse to take responsibility for
their actions at some time or other during their lives, and
some men so consistently shirk their duty that they present
more the appearance of overgrown children than of adults.
Inasmuch as moral autonomy is simply the condition of
taking full responsibility for one's actions, it follows that
men can forfeit their autonomy at will. That is to say, a
man can decide to obey the commands of another without
making any attempt to determine for himself whether
what is commanded is good or wise.

This is an important point, and it should not be confused with the false assertion that a man can give up responsibility for his actions. Evan after he has subjected
himself to the will of another, an individual remains responsible for what he does. But by refusing to engage in
moral deliberation, by accepting as final the commands of
the others, he forfeits his autonomy. Rousseau is therefore
right when he says that a man cannot become a slave even
through his own choice, if he means that even slaves are

morally responsible for their acts. But he is wrong if he means that men cannot place themselves voluntarily in a position of servitude and mindless obedience.

There are many forms and degrees of forfeiture of autonomy. A man can give up his independence of judgment with regard to a single question, or in respect of a single type of question. For example, when I place myself in the hands of my doctor, I commit myself to whatever course of treatment he prescribes, but only in regard to my health. I do not make him my legal counselor as well. A man may forfeit autonomy on some or all questions for a specific period of time, or during his entire life. He may submit himself to all commands, whatever they may be, save for some specified acts (such as killing) which he refuses to perform. From the example of the doctor, it is obvious that there are at least some situations in which it is reasonable to give up one's autonomy. Indeed, we may wonder whether, in a complex world of technical expertise, it is ever reasonable *not* to do so!

Since the concept of taking and forfeiting responsibility is central to the discussion which follows, it is worth devoting a bit more space to clarifying it. Taking responsibility for one's actions means making the final decisions about what one should do. For the autonomous man, there is no such thing, strictly speaking, as a *command*. If someone in my environment is issuing what are intended as commands, and if he or others expect those commands to be obeyed, that fact will be taken account of in my deliberations. I may decide that I ought to do what that person is commanding me to do, and it may even be that his issuing the command is the factor in the situation which makes it desirable for me to do so. For example, if I am on a sinking ship and the captain is giving orders for manning the life-boats, and if everyone else is obeying the captain *because he is the captain,* I may decide that under the circumstances I had better do what he says, since the confusion caused by disobeying him would be generally harmful. But insofar as I make such a decision, I am not *obeying his command*; that is, I am not acknowledging him as having authority over me. I would make the same decision, for exactly the same reasons, if one of the passengers had started to issue "orders" and had, in the confusion, come to be obeyed.

In politics, as in life generally, men frequently forfeit their autonomy. There are a number of causes for this fact, and also a number of arguments which have been offered to justify it. Most men, as we have already noted, feel so strongly the force of tradition or bureaucracy that they accept unthinkingly the claims to authority which are made by their nominal rulers. It is the rare individual in the history of the race who rises even to the level of questioning the right of his masters to command and the duty of himself and his fellows to obey. Once the dangerous question has been started, however, a variety of arguments can be brought forward to demonstrate the authority of the rulers. Among the most ancient is Plato's assertion that men should submit to the authority of those with superior knowledge, wisdom, or insight. A sophisticated modern version has it that the educated portion of a democratic population is more likely to be politically active, and that it is just as well for the ill-informed segment of the electorate to remain passive, since its entrance into the political arena only supports the efforts of demagogues and extremists. A number of American political scientists have gone so far as to claim that the apathy of the American masses is a cause of stability and hence a good thing.

The moral condition demands that we acknowledge responsibility and achieve autonomy wherever and whenever possible. Sometimes this involves moral deliberation and reflection; at other times, the gathering of special, even technical, information. The contemporary American citizen, for example, has an obligation to master enough modern science to enable him to follow debates about nuclear policy and come to an independent conclusion.[5] There are great, perhaps insurmountable, obstacles to the achievement of a complete and rational autonomy in the modern world. Nevertheless, so long as we recognize our responsibility for our actions, and acknowledge the power of reason within us, we must acknowledge as well the continuing obligation to make ourselves the authors of such commands as we may obey. The paradox of man's condition in the modern world is that the more fully he recognizes his right and duty to be his own master, the more completely he becomes the passive object of a technology and bureaucracy whose complexities he cannot hope to understand. It is only several hundred years since a reasonably well-educated man could claim to understand the major issues of government as well as his king or parliament. Ironically, the high school graduate of today, who

5. This is not quite so difficult as it sounds, since policy very rarely turns on disputes over technical or theoretical details. Still, the citizen who, for example, does not understand the nature of atomic radiation cannot even pretend to have an opinion on the feasibility of bomb shelters; and since the momentous choice between first-strike and second-strike nuclear strategies depends on the possibility of a successful shelter system, the uninformed citizen will be as completely at the mercy of his "representatives" as the lowliest slave.

cannot master the issues of foreign and domestic policy on which he is asked to vote, could quite easily have grasped the problems of eighteenth-century statecraft.

3. The Conflict Between Authority and Autonomy

The defining mark of the state is authority, the right to rule. The primary obligation of man is autonomy, the refusal to be ruled. It would seem, then, that there can be no resolution of the conflict between the autonomy of the individual and the putative authority of the state. Insofar as a man fulfills his obligation to make himself the author of his decisions, he will resist the state's claim to have authority over him. That is to say, he will deny that he has a duty to obey the laws of the state *simply because they are the laws.* In that sense, it would seem that anarchism is the only political doctrine consistent with the virtue of autonomy.

Now, of course, an anarchist may grant the necessity of *complying* with the law under certain circumstances or for the time being. He may even doubt that there is any real prospect of eliminating the state as a human institution. But he will never view the commands of the state as *legitimate,* as having a binding moral force. In a sense, we might characterize the anarchist as a man without a country, for despite the ties which bind him to the land of his childhood, he stands in precisely the same moral relationship to "his" government as he does to the government of any other country in which he might happen to be staying for a time. When I take a vacation in Great Britain, I obey its laws, both because of prudential self-interest and because of the obvious moral considerations concerning the value of order, the general good consequences of preserving a system of property, and so forth. On my return to the United States, I have a sense of reentering *my* country, and if I think about the matter at all, I imagine myself to stand in a different and more intimate relation to American laws. They have been promulgated by *my* government, and I therefore have a special obligation to obey them. But the anarchist tells me that my feeling is purely sentimental and has no objective moral basis. All authority is equally illegitimate, although of course not therefore equally worthy or unworthy of support, and my obedience to American laws, if I am to be morally autonomous, must proceed from the same considerations which determine me abroad.

The dilemma which we have posed can be succinctly expressed in terms of the concept of a *de jure* state. If all men have a continuing obligation to achieve the highest degree of autonomy possible, then there would appear to be no state whose subjects have a moral obligation to obey its commands. Hence, the concept of a *de jure* legitimate state would appear to be vacuous, and philosophical anarchism would seem to be the only reasonable political belief for an enlightened man.

II.
The Solution of
Classical Democracy

———◆—◆—◆———

1. Democracy Is the Only Feasible Solution

It is not necessary to argue at length the merits of all the various types of state which, since Plato, have been the standard fare of political philosophies. John Locke may have found it worthwhile to devote an entire treatise to Sir Robert Filmer's defense of the hereditary rights of kings, but today the belief in all forms of traditional authority is as weak as the arguments which can be given for it. There is only one form of political community which offers any hope of resolving the conflict between authority and autonomy, and that is democracy.

The argument runs thus: men cannot be free so long as they are subject to the will of others, whether one man (a monarch) or several (aristocrats). But if men rule themselves, if they are both law-givers and law-obeyers, then they can combine the benefits of government with the blessings of freedom. Rule *for* the people is merely benevolent slavery, but rule *by* the people is true freedom. Insofar as a man participates in the affairs of state, he is ruler as well as ruled. His obligation to submit to the laws stems not from the divine right of the monarch, nor from the hereditary authority of a noble class, but from the fact that he himself is the source of the laws which govern him. Therein lies the peculiar merit and moral claim of a democratic state.

Democracy attempts a natural extension of the duty of autonomy to the realm of collective action. Just as the truly responsible man gives laws to himself, and thereby binds himself to what he conceives to be right, so a society of responsible men can collectively bind themselves to laws collectively made, and thereby bind themselves to what they have together judged to be right. The government of a democratic state is then, strictly speaking, no more than a servant of the people as a whole, charged with the execution of laws which have been commonly agreed upon. In the words of Rousseau, "every person, while uniting himself with all, ... obey[s] only himself and remain[s] as free as before" (*Social Contract,* Bk. I, Ch. 6).

Let us explore this proposal more closely. We shall begin with the simplest form of democratic state, which may be labeled *unanimous direct democracy*.

2. Unanimous Direct Democracy

There is, in theory, a solution to the problem which has been posed, and this fact is in itself quite important. However, the solution requires the imposition of impossibly restrictive conditions which make it applicable only to a rather bizarre variety of actual situations. The solution is a direct democracy—that is, a political community in which every person votes on every issue—governed by a rule of unanimity. Under unanimous direct democracy, every member of the society wills freely every law which is actually passed. Hence, he is only confronted as a citizen with laws to which he has consented. Since a man who is constrained only by the dictates of his own will is autonomous, it follows that under the directions of unanimous direct democracy, men can harmonize the duty of autonomy with the commands of authority.

It might be argued that even this limiting case is not genuine, since each man is obeying himself, and hence is not submitting to a legitimate authority. However, the case is really different from the prepolitical (or extrapolitical) case of self-determination, for the authority to which each citizen submits is not that of himself simply, but that of the entire community taken collectively. The laws are issued in the name of the sovereign, which is to say the total population of the community. The power which enforces the law (should there be any citizen who, having voted for a law, now resists its application to himself) is the power of all, gathered together into the police power of the state. By this means, the moral conflict between duty and interest which arises from time to time within each man is externalized, and the voice of duty now speaks with the authority of law. Each man, in a manner of speaking, encounters his better self in the form of the state, for its dictates are simply the laws which he has, after due deliberation, willed to be enacted.

Unanimous direct democracy is feasible only so long as

there is substantial agreement among *all* the members of a community on the matters of major importance. Since by the rule of unanimity a single negative vote defeats any motion, the slightest disagreement over significant questions will bring the operations of the society to a halt. It will cease to function as a political community and fall into a condition of anarchy (or at least into a condition of non-legitimacy; a *de facto* government may of course emerge and take control). However, it should not be thought that unanimous direct democracy requires for its existence a perfect harmony of the interests or desires of the citizens. It is perfectly consistent with such a system that there be sharp, even violent, oppositions within the community, perhaps of an economic kind. The only necessity is that when the citizens come together to deliberate on the means for resolving such conflicts, they agree unanimously on the laws to be adopted.[6]

For example, a community may agree unanimously on some principles of compulsory arbitration by which economic conflicts are to be settled. An individual who has voted for these principles may then find himself personally disadvantaged by their application in a particular case. Thinking the principles fair, and knowing that he voted for them, he will (hopefully) acknowledge his moral obligation to accept their operation even though he would

6. In recent years, a number of political philosophers have explored the possibilities of decision by unanimity, and it turns out that much more can be achieved than one would expect. For example, John Rawls, in an influential and widely read essay, "Justice as Fairness," uses certain models taken from bargaining theory to analyze the conditions under which rational men with conflicting interests might arrive at unanimous agreement on the procedural principles for resolving their disputes. See Rawls in *Philosophy, Politics, and Society,* 2nd series, eds. P. Laslett and W. Runciman.

dearly like not to be subject to them. He will recognize
the principles as his own, just as any of us who has committed himself to a moral principle will, uncomfortably to
be sure, recognize its binding force upon him even when it
is inconvenient. More precisely, this individual will have
a moral obligation to obey the commands of the mediation
board or arbitration council, *whatever it decides,* because
the principles which guide it issue from his own will. Thus
the board will have authority over him (i.e., a right to be
obeyed) while he retains his moral autonomy.

Under what circumstances might a unanimous direct
democracy actually function for a reasonable period of
time without simply coming to a series of negative decisions? The answer, I think, is that there are two sorts of
practical unanimous direct democracies. First, a community of persons inspired by some all-absorbing religious
or secular ideal might find itself so completely in agreement on the goals of the community and the means for
achieving them that decisions could be taken on all major
questions by a method of consensus. Utopian communities
in the nineteenth century and some of the Israeli kib-
butzim in the twentieth are plausible instances of such a
functioning unanimity. Eventually, the consensus dissolves
and factions appear, but in some cases the unanimity has
been preserved for a period of many years.

Second, a community of rationally self-interested individuals may discover that it can only reap the fruits of cooperation by maintaining unanimity. So long as each member
of the community remains convinced that the benefits
to him from cooperation—even under the conditions of
compromise imposed by the need for unanimity—outweigh
the benefits of severing his connection with the rest, the

community will continue to function. For example, a classical laissez-faire economy ruled by the laws of the marketplace is supposedly endorsed by all the participants because each one recognizes *both* that he is better off in the system than out *and* that any relaxation of the ban against arrangements in restraint of trade would in the end do him more harm than good. So long as every businessman believes these two propositions, there will be unanimity on the laws of the system despite the cutthroat competition.[7]

As soon as disagreement arises on important questions, unanimity is destroyed and the state must either cease to be *de jure* or else discover some means for settling disputed issues which does not deprive any member of his autonomy. Furthermore, when the society grows too large for convenience in calling regular assemblies, some way must be found to conduct the business of the state without condemning most of the citizens to the status of voiceless subjects. The traditional solutions in democratic theory to these familiar problems are of course majority rule and representation. Our next task, therefore, is to discover whether representative majoritarian democracy preserves the autonomy which men achieve under a unanimous direct democracy.

Since unanimous democracy can exist only under such limited conditions, it might be thought that there is very little point in discussing it at all. For two reasons, however,

7. Strictly speaking, this second example of a viable unanimous community is imperfect, since there is a significant difference between committing oneself to a moral principle and calculating one's enlightened self-interest. For an illuminating discussion of the moral importance of committing oneself to a principle, see Rawls, *op. cit.*

unanimous direct democracy has great theoretical importance. First, it *is* a genuine solution to the problem of autonomy and authority, and as we shall see, this makes it
rather unusual. More important still, unanimous direct
democracy is the (frequently unexpressed) ideal which
underlies a great deal of classical democratic theory. The
devices of majoritarianism and representation are introduced in order to overcome obstacles which stand in the
way of unanimity and direct democracy. Unanimity is
clearly thought to be the method of making decisions
which is most obviously legitimate; other forms are presented as compromises with this ideal, and the arguments
in favor of them seek to show that the authority of a
unanimous democracy is not fatally weakened by the necessity of using representation or majority rule. One evi-
dence of the theoretical primacy of unanimous direct
democracy is the fact that in all social contract theories,
the original collective adoption of the social contract is
always a unanimous decision made by everyone who can
later be held accountable to the new state. Then the various compromise devices are introduced as practical measures, and their legitimacy is derived from the legitimacy
of the original contract. The assumption that unanimity
creates a *de jure* state is usually not even argued for with
any vigor; it seems to most democratic theorists perfectly
obvious.

3. Representative Democracy

Although the problem of disagreement is the more immediate, I shall deal first with the difficulties of assembly

which lead—in democratic theory—to the device of a representative parliament.[8] There are two problems which are overcome by representation: first, the total citizenry may be too numerous to meet together in a chamber or open field; and second, the business of government may require a continuous attention and application which only the idle rich or the career politician can afford to give it.

We may distinguish a number of types of representation, ranging from the mere delegation of the right to vote a proxy to a complete turning over of all decision-making functions. The question to be answered is whether any of these forms of representation adequately preserve the autonomy which men exercise through decisions taken unanimously by the entire community. In short, should a responsible man commit himself to obey the laws made by his representatives?

The simplest sort of representation is strict agency. If I am unable to attend the assembly at which votes are taken, I may turn over my proxy to an agent with instructions as to how to vote. In that case, it is obvious that I am as obligated by the decisions of the assembly as though I had been physically present. The role of legal agent is too narrowly drawn, however, to serve as an adequate model for an elected representative. In practice, it is impossible for representatives to return to their districts before each vote in the assembly and canvass their constituents. The citizens may of course arm their representative with a list of their preferences on future votes, but many of the issues which come before the assembly may not have been

8. Needless to say, the origin of parliaments historically has nothing to do with this problem. It is rather the other way around: first there were parliaments, then there was universal suffrage.

raised in the community at the time the representative was chosen. Unless there is to be a recall election on the occasion of each unforeseen deliberation, the citizens will be forced to choose as their representative a man whose general "platform" and political bent suggests that he will, in the future, vote as they imagine they would themselves, on issues which neither the citizens nor the representative yet have in mind.

When matters have reached this degree of removal from direct democracy, we may seriously doubt whether the legitimacy of the original arrangement has been preserved. I have an obligation to obey the laws which I myself enact. I have as well an obligation to obey the laws which are enacted by my agent in strict accord with my instructions. But on what grounds can it be claimed that I have an obligation to obey the laws which are made in my name by a man who has no obligation to vote as I would, who indeed has no effective way of discovering what my preferences are on the measure before him? Even if the parliament is unanimous in its adoption of some new measure, that fact can only bind the deputies and not the general citizenry who are said to be represented by them.

It can be replied that my obligation rests upon my *promise* to obey, and that may in fact be true. But insofar as a promise of that sort is the sole ground of my duty to obey, I can no longer be said to be *autonomous*. I have ceased to be the author of the laws to which I submit and have become the (willing) subject of another person. Precisely the same answer must be given to the argument that good effects of some sort will result from my obeying the duly elected parliament. The moral distinction of representative government, if there is any, does not lie in the general

good which it does, nor in the fact that its subjects have
consented to be ruled by a parliament. Benevolent elective
kingship of a sort which has existed in past societies can
say as much. The special legitimacy and moral authority of
representative government is thought to result from its being an expression of the will of the people whom it rules.
Representative democracy is said not simply to be government *for* the people but also government (indirectly) *by*
the people. I must obey what the parliament enacts, *whatever that may be,* because its will is my will, its decisions
my decisions, and hence its authority merely the collected
authority of myself and my fellow citizens. Now, a parliament whose deputies vote without specific mandate from
their constituents is no more the expression of their will
than is a dictatorship which rules with kindly intent but
independently of its subjects. It does not matter that I am
pleased with the outcome after the fact, nor even that my
representative has voted as he imagines I would have liked
him to. So long as I do not, either in person or through my
agent, join in the enactment of the laws by which I am
governed, I cannot justly claim to be autonomous.

Unfounded as is traditional representative government's
claim to the mantle of legitimacy, it seems impeccable in
comparison with the claims of the form of "democratic"
politics which actually exist in countries like the United
States today. Since World War II, governments have in-
creasingly divorced themselves in their decision-making
from anything which could be called the will of the people.
The complexity of the issues, the necessity of technical
knowledge, and most important, the secrecy of everything
having to do with national security, have conspired to at-
tenuate the representative function of elected officials un-

til a point has been reached which might be called political stewardship, or, after Plato, "elective guardianship." The President of the United States is merely pledged to serve the unspecified interests of his constituents in unspecified ways.

The right of such a system to the title of democracy is customarily defended by three arguments: first, the rulers are chosen by the people from a slate which includes at least two candidates for each office; second, the rulers are expected to act in what they conceive to be the interest of the people; and third, the people periodically have the opportunity to recall their rulers and select others. More generally, the system allows individuals to have some measurable influence on the ruling elite if they choose. The genealogy of the term "democracy" need not concern us. It suffices to note that the system of elective guardianship falls so far short of the ideal of autonomy and self-rule as not even to seem a distant deviation from it. Men cannot meaningfully be called free if their representatives vote independently of their wishes, or when laws are passed concerning issues which they are not able to understand. Nor can men be called free who are subject to secret decisions, based on secret data, having unannounced consequences for their well-being and their very lives.

Some while after John Kennedy was assassinated, several memoirs appeared recounting the inside story of the decisions to invade Cuba in 1961 and to risk a nuclear war by blockading Cuba in 1962. More recently, with the advent of the Nixon Administration, we have begun to learn something of the way in which President Johnson and his advisers committed this country to a massive land war in Vietnam. As this book is being prepared for publication, new decisions are being taken in secret which may involve the United States in the Laotian situation.

In none of these instances of major decisions is there the slightest relation between the real reasons determining official policy and the rationale given out for public consumption. In what way, it may be wondered, are Americans better off than those Russian subjects who were allowed, by Khrushchev's decision, to know a bit of the truth about Stalin?

Even those forms of representative government which approximate to genuine agency suffer from a curious and little-noted defect which robs electors of their freedom to determine the laws under which they shall live. The assumption which underlies the practice of representation is that the individual citizen has an opportunity, through his vote, to make his preference known. Leaving aside for the moment the problems connected with majority rule, and ignoring as well the derogations from legitimacy which result when issues are voted on in the parliament which were not canvassed during the election of deputies, the citizen who makes use of his ballot is, as it were, present in the chamber through the agency of his representative. But this assumes that at the time of the election, each man had a genuine opportunity to vote for a candidate who represented his point of view. He may find himself in the minority, of course; his candidate may lose. But at least he has had his chance to advance his preferences at the polls.

But if the number of issues under debate during the campaign is greater than one or two, and if there are—as there are sure to be—a number of plausible positions which might be taken on each issue, then the permutations of consistent alternative total "platforms" will be vastly greater than the number of candidates. Suppose, for example, that in an American election there are four issues: a farm bill, medical care for the aged, the extension of the draft, and civil rights. Simplifying the real world considerably, we can suppose that there are three alternative courses of action seriously being considered on the first issue, four on the second, two on the third, and three on the last. There are then $3 \times 4 \times 2 \times 3 = 72$ possible stands which a man might take on these four issues. For example, he might favor full parity, Kerr-Mills, discontinuation of the draft, and no civil rights bill; or free market on agricultural produce, no medicare at all, extension of the draft, and a strong civil rights bill; and so on. Now, in order to make sure that every voter has a *chance* of voting for what he believes, there would have to be 72 candidates, each holding one of the logically possible positions. If a citizen cannot even find a *candidate* whose views coincide with his own, then there is no possibility at all that he will send to the parliament a genuine *representative*. In practice, voters are offered a handful of candidates and must make compromises with their beliefs before they ever get to the polls. Under these circumstances, it is difficult to see what content there is to the platitude that elections manifest the will of the people.

The most biting rejection of representative democracy can be found in Rousseau's *Social Contract*. In opposition to such writers as Locke, Rousseau writes:

> Sovereignty cannot be represented for the same reason that it cannot be alienated; its essence is the general will, and that will must speak for itself or it does not exist: it is either itself or not itself: there is no intermediate possibility. The deputies of the people, there-

fore, are not and cannot be their representatives; they can only be their commissioners, and as such are not qualified to conclude anything definitively. No act of theirs can be a law, unless it has been ratified by the people in person; and without that ratification nothing is a law. The people of England deceive themselves when they fancy they are free; they are so, in fact, only during the election of members of parliament: for, as soon as a new one is elected, they are again in chains, and are nothing. And thus, by the use they make of their brief moments of liberty, they deserve to lose it (Bk. III, Ch. 15).

APPENDIX: A PROPOSAL FOR INSTANT DIRECT DEMOCRACY

The practical impossibility of direct democracy is generally taken for granted in contemporary discussions of democratic theory, and it is accounted an unpleasantly utopian aspect of the philosophy of Rousseau, for example, that it assumes a community in which every citizen can vote directly on all the laws. Actually, the obstacles to direct democracy are merely technical, and we may therefore suppose that in this day of planned technological progress it is possible to solve them. The following proposal sketches one such solution. It is meant a good deal more than half in earnest, and I urge those readers who are prone to reject it out of hand to reflect on what that reaction reveals about their real attitude toward democracy.

I propose that in order to overcome the obstacles to direct democracy, a system of in-the-home voting machines be set up. In each dwelling, a device would be attached to the television set which would electronically record votes and transmit them to a computer in Washington. (Those homes without sets would be supplied by a federal subsidy. In practice this would not be very expensive, since only the very poor and the very intelligent lack sets at present.) In order to avoid fraudulent voting, the device could be rigged to record thumbprints. In that manner, each person would be able to vote only once, since the computer would automatically reject a duplicate vote. Each evening, at the time which is now devoted to news programs, there would be a nationwide all-stations show devoted to debate on the issues before the nation. Whatever bills were "before the Congress" (as we would now describe it) would be debated by representatives of alternative points of view. There would be background briefings on technically complex questions, as well as formal debates, question periods, and so forth. Committees of experts would be commissioned to gather data, make recommendations for new measures, and do the work of drafting legislation. One could institute the position of Public Dissenter in order to guarantee that dissident and unusual points of view were heard. Each Friday, after a week of debate and discussion, a voting session would be held. The measures would be put to the public, one by one, and the nation would record its preference instantaneously by means of the machines. Special arrangements might have to be made for those who could not be at their sets during the voting. (Perhaps voting sessions at various times during the preceding day and night.) Simple majority rule would prevail, as is now the case in the Congress.

The proposal is not perfect, of course, for there is a great difference between the passive role of listener in a debate and the active role of participant. Nevertheless, it should

be obvious that a political community which conducted its
business by means of "instant direct democracy" would be
immeasurably closer to realizing the ideal of genuine democracy than we are in any so-called democratic country
today. The major objection which would immediately be
raised to the proposal, particularly by American political
scientists, is that it would be too democratic! What chaos
would ensue! What anarchy would prevail! The feckless
masses, swung hither and yon by the winds of opinion,
would quickly reduce the great, slow-moving, stable government of the United States to disorganized shambles!
Bills would be passed or unpassed with the same casual
irresponsibility which now governs the length of a hemline
or the popularity of a beer. Meretricious arguments would
delude the simple, well-meaning, ignorant folk into voting
for pie-in-the-sky giveaways; foreign affairs would swing
between jingoist militarism and craven isolationism. Gone
would be the restraining hand of wisdom, knowledge, tradition, experience.

The likelihood of responses of this sort indicates the
shallowness of most modern belief in democracy. It is obvious that very few individuals really hold with *government
by the people,* though of course we are all willing to oblit-
erate ourselves and our enemies in its name. Nevertheless, the unbelievers are, in my opinion, probably wrong
as well as untrue to their professed faith. The initial response to a system of instant direct democracy would be
chaotic, to be sure. But very quickly, men would learn—
what is now manifestly not true—that their votes made a
difference in the world, an immediate, visible difference.
There is nothing which brings on a sense of responsibility
so fast as that awareness. America would see an immediate

and invigorating rise in interest in politics. It would hardly be necessary to launch expensive and frustrating campaigns to get out the vote. Politics would be on the lips of every man, woman, and child, day after day. As interest rose, a demand would be created for more and better sources of news. Even under the present system, in which very few Americans have any sense of participation in politics, news is so popular that quarter-hour programs are expanded to half an hour, and news specials preempt prime television time. Can anyone deny that instant direct democracy would generate a degree of interest and participation in political affairs which is now considered impossible to achieve?

Under a system of genuine democracy the voices of the many would drown out those of the few. The poor, the uneducated, the frightened who today are cared for by the state on occasion but never included in the process of government would weigh, man for man, as heavily as the rich, the influential, the well-connected. Much might be endangered that is worthwhile by such a system, but at least social justice would flourish as it has never flourished before.

If we are willing to think daringly, then, the practical obstacles to direct democracy can be overcome. For the moment, we need not discuss any further *whether* we wish to overcome them; but since our investigation concerns the *possibility* of establishing a state in which the autonomy of the individual is compatible with the authority of the state, I think we can take it that the difficulties which in the past have led to unsatisfactory forms of representative democracy do not constitute a serious theoretical problem.

4. Majoritarian Democracy

The principal theoretical weakness of unanimous direct democracy is its requirement that decisions be taken unanimously in order for them to acquire the authority of law. As a practical matter, of course, this requirement severely limits the actual situations in which a state can flourish, but it is perhaps an even more serious failing of unanimous democracy that it offers no way at all for men of good will to resolve their differences. Presumably, in order for the concept of a just state to have more than idle interest, it must at least in theory be possible for conflicts to be resolved without a loss of autonomy on the part of the citizens or of authority on the part of the state. The conflicts need not be motivated by divisive self-interest; they may simply be disagreements over the best way to pursue the common good.

The solution which immediately springs to the fore is, of course, majority rule. Where the electorate are divided, take a vote; give to each man one vote, and let the group as a whole be committed by the preponderance of voices. So widespread is the belief in majority rule that there is not a single variant of democratic theory which does not call upon it as the means for composing differences and arriving at decisions. Our task is to discover an argument which demonstrates that the autonomy of unanimous democracy is preserved in a democracy which is guided by the rule of the majority. In other words, we must inquire whether the members of a democratic polity are morally bound to obey the decisions of the majority, and if so, why.

The problem, of course, concerns those who find themselves in the minority on any question. The members of the majority bear the same relation to the law they have passed as do all the citizens in a unanimous democracy. Since the majority have willed the law, they are bound by it, and they remain autonomous in submitting to its authority. A member of the minority, however, has voted against the law, and he appears to be in the position of a man who, deliberating on a moral question, rejects an alternative only to find it forced upon him by a superior power. His readiness to deliberate, and to be committed by his decision, manifests his desire to be autonomous; but insofar as he must submit to the will of the majority, it seems that his desire is frustrated.

One common justification of majority rule is that, on prudential or general moral grounds, it works better than any other system which has been devised. For example, it is said that democratic politics is a substitute for the rule of arms which prevails in lawless societies. Since the majority are, militarily speaking, likely to be the superior body, they must be allowed to rule by the ballot; for otherwise they will resort to force and throw society back into chaos. Or, again, historical observation may reveal that rule by the majority tends to advance the general welfare better than any other system of government (such as rule by the wise or the powerful), since contrary to what Plato and others have supposed, the people know their own interest best. Majoritarian democracy, it is said, is therefore the most effective safeguard against the rule of a hypocritically self-interested elite. From the point of view of the individual, it might be urged that submission to the rule of the majority offers him the best chance, in the long run, for advancing his own interests, since by and large he will find himself in the majority as often as in the minority, and the benefit flowing from collective action will outweigh the losses suffered when his side loses.

All such defenses, and others besides which might be based on considerations of interest or good consequences, are, however, strictly irrelevant to our inquiry. As justifications for an individual's autonomous decision to cooperate with the state, they may be perfectly adequate; but as demonstrations of the *authority* of the state—as proofs, that is, of the right of the state to command the individual and of his obligation to obey, *whatever may be commanded*—they fail completely. If the individual retains his autonomy by reserving to himself in each instance the final decision whether to cooperate, he thereby denies the authority of the state; if, on the other hand, he submits to the state and accepts its claim to authority, then so far as any of the above arguments indicate, he loses his autonomy.

Indeed, the prudential and casuistical defenses of democracy do not succeed in distinguishing it morally from any other form of political community. A man might find that his affairs flourished in a dictatorship or monarchy, and even that the welfare of the people as a whole was effectively advanced by the policies of such a state. Democracy, then, could claim to be no more than one type of *de facto* government among many, and its virtues, if any, would be purely relative. Perhaps, as Winston Churchill once remarked, democracy is the worst form of government except for all the others; but if so, then the "citizens" of America are as much subjects of an alien power as the Spaniards under Franco or the Russians under Stalin. They are merely more fortunate in their rulers.

A more serious case for majority rule can be founded on the terms of the contract by which the political order is constituted. According to many theorists of democracy, the transition from unanimous rule, as exemplified by the adoption of the social contract, to majority rule, on which the subsequent functionings of the society depend, is provided for by a clause in the original agreement. Everyone pledges himself henceforth to abide by the rule of the majority, and whenever a citizen objects to being required to obey laws for which he has not voted, he can be recalled to his promise. On that pact, it is asserted, rests the moral authority of a majoritarian state.[9]

But this argument is no better than the previous one. A promise to abide by the will of the majority creates an obligation, *but it does so precisely by giving up one's autonomy*. It is perfectly possible to forfeit autonomy, as we have already seen. Whether it is wise, or good, or right to do so is, of course, open to question, but *that* one can do so is obvious. Hence, if citizens contract to govern themselves by majority rule, they thereby obligate themselves in just

9. A great deal has been written, in mitigation of the manifest historical implausibility of contract theories, about the metaphorical or mythical character of the original "contract." Sometimes, for example, it is said that the contract merely states in convenient form the underlying moral consensus of the society. It should be clear that a sophisticated interpretation of this sort will not do, if one wishes to found majority rule on the promise contained in the' contract. A promise is an act, not the mere expression or summation of an existing obligation. It creates a new obligation where none existed before. Whatever may be my general moral obligation to do an act, my promise to do it lays an independent burden of responsibility upon me. Hence, those theorists who trace the legitimacy of majoritarianism to the contract cannot, in all consistency, dissolve the contract into a myth. Needless to say, there can be tacit promises as well as explicit promises, and therefore tacit or quasi-contracts of the sort which are invoked to explain the obligation of succeeding generations.

the manner that they would be obligated by any promise. The state then has a right to command them, assuming that it is guided only by the majority. But the citizens have created a legitimate state at the price of their own autonomy! They have bound themselves to obey laws which they do not will, and indeed even laws which they vigorously reject. Insofar as democracy originates in such a promise, it is no more than voluntary slavery, and the characterization which Rousseau gives of the English form of representation can as well be applied here.

The force of this point is difficult to grasp, for we are so deeply imbued with the ethic of majoritarianism that it possesses for us the deceptive quality of self-evidence. In the United States, little children are taught to let the majority rule almost before they are old enough to count the votes. Whenever force or wealth threatens to dominate a situation, the voice of the majority is appealed to as the higher call of morality and reason. Not rule by the majority? What else is there, one wants to ask. Perhaps it will help, therefore, to reflect that the justification of majority rule by appeal to an original promise opens the way to justification of virtually any other mode of decision-making, for the contracting citizens could as well have promised to abide by minority rule, or random choice, or the rule of a monarch, or rule by the best educated, or rule by the least educated, or even rule by a daily dictator chosen by lot.

If the only argument for majority rule is its legitimation by unanimous vote at the founding convention, then presumably *any* method of decision-making at all which was given that sanction would be equally legitimate. If we hold that majority rule has some special validity, then it must be because of the character of majority rule itself, and not because of a promise which we may be thought to have made to abide by it. What is required, therefore, is a direct justification of majority rule itself, that is, a demonstration that under majority rule the minority do not forfeit their autonomy in submitting to the decisions of the collectivity.

John Locke somewhat recognizes the necessity for a proof of the principle of majority rule, and at the very outset of his *Second Treatise Concerning Civil Government* offers the following:

> When any number of men have so consented to make one community or government, they are thereby presently incorporated, and make one body politic, wherein the majority have a right to act and conclude the rest. For when any number of men have, by the consent of every individual, made a community, they have thereby made that community one body, with a power to act as one body, which is only by the will and determination of the majority. For that which acts [i.e., activates] any community being only the consent of the individuals of it, and it being one body must move one way, it is necessary the body should move that way whither the greater force carries it, which is the consent of the majority; or else it is impossible it should act or continue one body, one community, which the consent of every individual that united into it agreed that it should; and so every one is bound by that consent to be concluded by the majority (Ch. VIII).

The key to the argument is the assertion that the body politic must be carried "whither the greater force carries it." If this means that the state *must in fact* move in the direction of the preponderance of power, it is either trivially true, power being defined by its effects, or else nontrivial and false, since frequently a minority can dominate the conduct of public affairs even though they command far less than a preponderance of the available force in the society. On the other hand, if Locke means that the state *ought* to move in the direction of the greater *moral* force, then presumably he believes that the majority will possess that superior moral force because each individual counts for one in the moral calculus. However, even if sense can be made of the notion of a moral force, we are still without a reason why the minority has an obligation to obey the majority.

One possible line of argument is to found the rule of the majority on the higher principle that each person in the society should have an equal chance to make his preferences the law. Assuming for the moment that the principle of equal chance is valid, does majority rule achieve that equality?

It is difficult to decide, since the notion of having an equal chance of making one's preferences law is ambiguous. In one sense, majority rule *guarantees* to the members of the majority that their preference will become law. Hence if a man knows that he is in the minority, he will realize that he has *no* chance at all of effecting his will. This is the characteristic of majoritarian democracy which drives permanent minorities into rebellion, and permits what Mill quite justly called the tyranny of the majority. A system of legislation by lot might therefore be more in accord with the principle of equal chance. Each individual could write his preference on a piece of paper, and the winning law could be drawn from a twirling basket. Then, we might suppose, each citizen could have exactly the same chance that his will would become law. But probability is a tricky science, and here again we must pause to reconsider. Each citizen, to be sure, would have the same chance for his piece of paper to be drawn from the basket; but presumably what he desires is simply that the law which he prefers be enacted, not that the enactment take place by means of his personal slip of paper. In other words, he would be equally satisfied by a drawing of *any* piece of paper on which his preference was written. Now, if there are more slips with alternative A on them than with alternative B, then of course the probability is higher of alternative A being chosen. Thus, legislation by lot would offer some chance to the minority, unlike rule by the majority, but it would not offer to each citizen an equal chance that his preference be enacted. Nevertheless, it does seem to come closer to the ideal of equal chances than majority rule.

We have cited the device of decision by random choice chiefly as a way of exposing the weaknesses of a certain justification of majority rule, but before going on to yet another argument for majoritarianism, it might be well to consider whether random decision is a worthy candidate for adoption in its own right. Is it reasonable to resolve differences of opinion by chance? Does commitment to such a device preserve the autonomy of the individual citizen, even when the die is cast against him?

We must not be too hasty in rejecting the appeal to chance, for in at least some situations of choice it would appear to be the proper method. For example, if I am faced with a choice among alternatives whose probable outcomes I cannot estimate, then it is perfectly sensible to let chance decide my choice. If I am lost in the forest, with not the slightest idea which direction is most promising, and if I am convinced that my best chance is to choose one path and stick to it, then I might as well spin myself around with my eyes closed and start off in any direction. More generally, it is reasonable to choose at random among equally promising alternatives.[10] Random decision is also reasonable in another sort of case, where rewards or burdens are to be distributed among equally deserving (or undeserving) citizens, and the nature of the item to be distributed makes it impossible to divide it and parcel out equal shares. Thus, if the armed forces require only one-half of the available men, and cannot adjust matters by halving the service time and doubling the draft, then the fair method of choosing inductees is to put the names in a bowl and pull them out at random.

Since the duty of autonomy dictates only that I use all *available* information in making my decisions, it is clear that randomization in the face of ignorance is not a derogation of autonomy. This is equally true in the second case, of indivisible payoffs, though we are there obligated to attempt to overcome the inevitable unfairness by incorporating the matter into a broader context and balancing off future rewards and burdens. It follows that the use of ran-

10. I am deliberately glossing over the much more controversial question, whether it is reasonable to equate a less probable outcome having a high value to me with a more probable outcome having a low value. Somewhat more technically, the question is whether I ought to be guided by my calculation of the expected value, or mathematical expectation, of the alternatives open to me. Von Neumann and Morgenstern, in their development of the pure theory of games, assume the rationality of maximization of expected value, but there is nothing approaching consensus on the issue in the contemporary literature.

dom devices in some collective decision will not violate autonomy, assuming for the moment that there has been unanimous agreement on their adoption. But what shall we say of the decision by lot in cases where the obstacle to decision is simple disagreement among the members of the assembly, and not ignorance of future outcomes or the indivisibility of payoffs? Is this, perhaps, a solution to the problem of the subjection of the minority?

In the making of individual decisions, an appeal to chance when the necessary information was at hand would be a willful forfeiture of autonomy. May we then conclude that the same is true for collective decision? Not so, it might be argued. If we are permitted, without loss of autonomy, to bow to the constraints of ignorance, or to the intractability of nature, why may we not with equal justification adjust ourselves to the limitations of collective as opposed to individual decision-making? When the assembly of the people cannot reach a unanimous decision, decision by lot is the only way to avoid the twin evils of governmental inertia and tyrannization of the minority.

This argument seems to me to be wrong, although my reasons for this belief will only be spelled out with any fullness in the last section of this essay. Briefly, there is a fundamental difference between those obstacles to decision which are outside our control, such as ignorance, and those obstacles which are at least theoretically within our control, such as psychological conflict (in the individual) or disagreement (in the society as a whole). Whereas we have no reason to think that we could ever completely overcome natural obstacles, even in an ideal society, we must suppose that some method exists for resolving conflicts among rational men of good will which allows them to concert their activities without forfeiting their autonomy. The general adoption of decision by lot would violate the autonomy of the citizens.

The most ambitious defense of majoritarianism in the literature of democratic theory is that offered by Jean-Jacques Rousseau in Book IV of the *Social Contract*. The fundamental problem of political philosophy, according to Rousseau, is to discover whether there is "a form of association which will defend and protect with the whole common force the person and the property of each associate, and by which every person, while uniting himself with all, shall obey only himself and remain as free as before."[11] The solution to this problem is the social contract by which men first constitute themselves a polity. By means of the contract, the many particular and divisive wills of the prepolitical community are transformed into the general will of the collective body. Each contracting party pledges himself to "place in common his person and all his power under the supreme direction of the general will; and as one body ... all receive each member as an indivisible part of the whole."

A will is distinguished by Rousseau as general by virtue both of its form and of its content, or aim. Formally, a will is general insofar as it issues in commands having the form of general law rather than particular edict. Thus, Rousseau considers only the laws of the society to be products of the general will; applications of the laws to particular

11. This is essentially the problem which I have called the deduction of the possibility of political philosophy. Rousseau appears to be the first political philosopher to recognize explicitly the conflict between the demands of moral autonomy and legitimate authority. My treatment of the problem owes a great deal to the *Social Contract*. (Bk. I, Ch. VI)

cases are made by the government, which operates under a mandate from the collective will of the people. Materially, a will is general insofar as it aims at the general good rather than at the particular goods of separate individuals. An individual can be said to have a general will, or to strive for a general will, if he aims at the general good rather than his own good, and if he issues commands having the form of law. Similarly, the group as a whole has a general will when it issues laws which aim at the general good. In this way, Rousseau distinguishes a true political community from an association of self-interested individuals who strike bargains among their competing interests, but nowhere strive for the good of the whole. (The same distinction is said to be embodied in the division of function between the Congress, which represents sectional and class interests, and the president, who is supposed to be guided by the national interest.)

It is Rousseau's claim that when a political community deliberates together on the general good and embodies its deliberations in general laws, it thereby acquires legitimate authority over all the members of the deliberating body, or parliament. Thenceforward, each member of the society has a moral obligation to obey the laws which have been willed by the collectivity. That obligation can be suspended only when the general will is destroyed, which is to say only if the parliament of all the people ceases to aim at the general good or to issue laws.

Rousseau, in keeping with the tradition of democratic theory, introduces the device of majority rule into the founding contract. But he recognizes that the legitimacy of laws enacted by a majority of the parliament cannot be traced merely to the binding force of a promise. In

Book IV of the *Social Contract,* therefore, he returns to the problem:

> Except in this original contract, a majority of the votes is sufficient to bind all the others. This is a consequence of the contract itself. But it may be asked how a man can be free and yet forced to conform to the will of others. How are the opposers free when they are in submission to laws to which they have never consented?

Rousseau continues:

> I answer that the question is not fairly stated. The citizen consents to all the laws, to those which are passed in spite of his opposition, and even to those which sentence him to punishment if he violates any one of them. The constant will of all the members of the State is the general will; it is by that they are citizens and free. When any law is proposed to the assembly of the people, the question is not precisely to enquire whether they approve the proposition or reject it, but if it is conformable or not to the general will, which is their will. Each citizen, in giving his suffrage, states his mind on that question; and the general will is found by counting the votes. When, therefore, the motion which I opposed carries, it only proves to me that I was mistaken, and that what I believed to be the general will was not so. If my particular opinion had prevailed, I should have done what I was not willing to do, and consequently, I should not have been in a state of freedom.

The air of paradox which surrounds this passage has enticed or repelled students of Rousseau ever since the *Social Contract* appeared. The notion of man being "forced to be free," which was employed by later idealist political philosophers to justify the state's repression of the individual "in the interest of his own true self," can be traced to this argument. Actually, as I shall try to show, there are no sinister implications to Rousseau's argument, although it is not valid.

The foundation of the argument is a distinction, whose lineage runs at least to Plato, between doing what one wills and doing what one wants. An individual may be said to do what he wills so long as he manages to perform the action which he sets out to perform; but he may thereby fail to do what he wants, if the outcome of the action is other than he anticipated. For example, suppose that I arrive at a train station just as my train is scheduled to leave. Not knowing which track I am to leave from, I rush up to a conductor and shout, "Which track for Boston?" He points at track 6, but I misunderstand him and dash off for track 5, where a train for Philadelphia is also on the point of leaving. The conductor, seeing my mistake, has only two choices: he can allow me to board the wrong train, thereby permitting me to do what I will, or bodily hustle me onto the right train, thereby forcing me to do what I want. Rousseau's description seems perfectly apposite. If the conductor makes no move to stop me, I will fail to do what I want to do, and in that sense not be free.

Consider another case, that of an intern who is on duty in the emergency ward of a hospital. A case comes in which he misdiagnoses as poisoning. He orders a stomach pump, which is about to be applied when the resident in charge happens by, recognizes the case as actually one of appendicitis, for which the stomach pump would be fatal, and countermands the intern's order to the nurse. Here, the intern's aim is of course to cure the patient, and he is as-

sisted in achieving it by the resident's counterorder, which
(in a manner of speaking) forces him to treat the patient
correctly. Had he been permitted to follow his own diag-
nosis, he would have accomplished precisely the end which
he most wished to avoid.

Plato, it will be recalled, uses this same argument in
the *Gorgias* and *Republic* in order to demonstrate that the
tyrant is not truly powerful. The tyrant, like all men, wants
what is good for him. Power, then, is the ability to get
what is good for oneself. But the tyrant, through a defect
of true moral knowledge, mistakenly thinks that it is good
for him to indulge his appetites, deal unjustly with his fellow men, and subordinate his rational faculties to his un-
checked desire and will. As a result, he becomes what we
would today call a neurotic individual; he compulsively
pursues fantasy-goals whose achievement gives him no real
happiness, and he thereby shows himself to be truly powerless to get what he wants.

The three cases of the man catching a train, the intern
diagnosing a patient, and the tyrant have three common
characteristics on which are founded the distinction between getting what one wills and getting what one wants.
First, it is supposedly quite easy to distinguish between the
goal of the individual's action and the means which he
adopts to achieve it. (This is, of course, debatable in the
case of the tyrant; it would hardly be denied in the other
cases.) Hence, we can speak meaningfully of the agent's
willing the means and wanting the end, and therefore of
his doing what he wills but failing to get what he wants.
Second, the goal in each case is some state of affairs whose
existence is objectively ascertainable, and about which one
can have knowledge. (Again, Plato's example is open to

dispute; this is precisely the point in the development of his ethical theory at which he makes use of the doctrine that there is such a thing as moral knowledge.) It follows that a man may sometimes know less well what he really wants (i.e., what will really accomplish his own goals) than some independent observer. Finally, in all three cases we are to assume that the individual places a purely instrumental value on the means which he adopts, and would be willing to give them up if he believed that they were ill suited to his ends.

Life is full of significant situations in which we strive to achieve some objective state of affairs, and in which we would therefore be sorry if our mistaken views about the means to those ends were to be adopted. For example, if a member of Congress genuinely wishes to reduce unemployment, and if his traditionalistic convictions about the virtues of a balanced budget are overriden by a liberal majority which seeks to spend the nation into prosperity, *and if unemployment is thereupon reduced,* then (personal pride to one side) we may expect him to be glad that his views were in the minority, for he can now see that "if his particular opinion had prevailed, he should have done what he was not willing to do, and consequently, he should not have been in a state of freedom."

And we can now see what Rousseau intended in the passage quoted above. He assumes that the assembly of the people is attempting to issue commands which have the form of law and aim at the general good. This is a legitimate assumption for Rousseau to make, since he is only interested in discovering whether a community which *does* aim at the general good thereby confers legitimacy on the laws which it passes. The further question, whether one can often find an assembly which holds to the ideal of the general good instead of pursuing diverse particular interests, concerns the application of Rousseau's theory. Democratic theorists frequently devote great attention to the problem of devising safeguards against the ineradicable partisanship of even the most enlightened men. Although that is indeed a serious matter, their concern tends to mask their unexamined assumption that a majoritarian democracy of thoroughly public-spirited citizens, if it ever could exist, would possess legitimate authority. This is merely one more reflection of the universal conviction that majority rule is self-evidently legitimate. By recognizing the necessity for an independent justification of majority rule, Rousseau plays in political philosophy the role which Hume plays in the theory of knowledge.

Rousseau supposes further that it is an objectively ascertainable fact whether a proposed law has the proper form and aims at the general good. He thinks, finally, that the proper test of these matters is a vote, in which the majority must inevitably be correct. Hence, when a member of the assembly "gives his suffrage," he is not expressing his *preference*, but rather offering his opinion on the character of the proposed law. He may perfectly well prefer a different measure, which serves his interest better, and nevertheless vote for the proposal because he believes it to aim at the general good. Since the majority are always right, a member of the minority will *by that fact* be revealed as supporting inappropriate means to his own end; in short, the minority are like the individual who dashes for the wrong train, or the intern who prescribes the wrong treatment.

The flaw in this argument, of course, is the apparently

groundless assumption that the majority are always right in their opinion concerning the general good. (Rousseau's appeal to this assumption is contained in the innocuous-looking words "and the general will is found by counting the votes.") What can possibly have led Rousseau to such an implausible conclusion? Experience would seem rather to suggest that truth lies with the minority in most disputes, and certainly that is the case in the early stages of the acceptance of new discoveries. At any rate, if the nature of the general good is a matter of knowledge, then there would appear to be no ground for assuming that the majority opinion on any particular proposal for the general good will inevitably be correct.

I think we can trace Rousseau's error to a pair of complicated confusions. First, Rousseau has not adequately distinguished between an assembly which attempts to aim at the general good, and one which actually succeeds. In a chapter entitled "Whether the General Will Can Err," he writes:

> It follows from what has been said that the general will is always right and tends always to the public advantage; but it does not follow that the deliberations of the people have always the same rectitude. Our will always seeks our own good, but we do not always perceive what it is. The people are never corrupted, but they are often deceived, and only then do they seem to will what is bad. (Bk. I, Ch. 3)

The confusion lies in failing to distinguish three possible conditions of the assembly. First, the citizenry may vote on the basis of private interest, in which case they are not even attempting to realize the general good. That is what

Rousseau calls an "aggregate will." Second, the people may strive to achieve the general good, but choose poor laws because of their ignorance, or simply the unpredictability of important aspects of the problems which they face. Insofar as everyone does his best to realize the general good, the collectivity is a genuine moral and political community. Finally, the assembly of the people may aim at the general good and hit it. They may deliberately choose to enact laws which do in fact offer the best way to achieve the good of the community.

Now, there may be some ground for claiming that an assembly which is in the second condition has legitimate authority over its members; one might argue that it acquires authority by virtue of the universal commitment of its members to the general good. But Rousseau's proof of the legitimacy of the majority will only work if we assume that the assembly is in the third condition—that whenever it is guided by the majority it actually succeeds in moving toward the general good. In that case, it really would be true that a member of the minority could get what he willed (the general good) only by failing to get what he voted for.

The confusion between trying to achieve the general good and succeeding is compounded, I would like to suggest, by a second confusion which leads Rousseau to overlook what would otherwise be a rather obvious error. There are three questions which one might suppose the assembly to be presented with. Rousseau mentions two: Which law do you prefer? and Which law tends to the general good? A third question might also be asked: Which alternative will win? Now the peculiarity of this last question is that the majority opinion *must be correct*. If everyone's vote is a prediction about the outcome, then the members of the minority will hardly desire their choice to prevail, for by so doing they would violate the principle of majority rule to which they are presumably committed. The phrase "general will" is ambiguous in Rousseau's usage, even though he takes great care to define it earlier in his essay. It should mean "will issuing laws which aim at the general good," but it frequently has for him the more ordinary meaning "preponderant opinion" or "consensus of the group." When the assembly is asked "whether (the proposition before them) is conformable or not to the general will," we may view them either as being asked for their opinion of the value of the proposition for the general good, or else as being asked to make a prediction of the outcome of the vote. I suggest that Rousseau himself confused these two senses, and was thereby led into the manifestly false assumption that the majority opinion of the assembly would successfully express what the minority were really striving for, and hence be binding on everyone who voted for or against.

We appear to be left with no plausible reason for believing that a direct democracy governed by majority rule preserves the moral autonomy of the individual while conferring legitimate authority on the sovereign. The problem remains, that those who submit to laws against which they have voted are no longer autonomous, even though they may have submitted voluntarily. The strongest argument for the moral authority of a majoritarian government is that it is founded upon the unanimous promise of obedience of its subjects. If such a promise may be supposed to exist, then the government does indeed have a moral right to command. But we have discovered no *moral* reason why men should by their promise bring a democratic state into being, and thereby forfeit their autonomy. The implicit claim of all democratic theory, I repeat, is that it offers a solution to the problem of combining moral liberty (autonomy) with political authority. This claim is justified for the special case of unanimous direct democracy. But none of the arguments which we have considered thus far succeed in demonstrating that this claim is also valid for majoritarian democracy.

This is not to deny that there are many other reasons for favoring democracy of one sort or another under the conditions which prevail today in advanced industrial societies. For example, one might reply impatiently to all the foregoing argumentation that majority rule seems to work well enough, and that minorities do not show signs of feeling trampled upon, for all that they may be frustrated or disappointed. To which one need only reply that the psychology of politics is not at issue here. Men's feelings of loss of autonomy, like their feelings of loyalty, are determined by such factors as the relative degree of satisfaction and frustration of deeply held desires which they experience. Modern interest-group democracy is, under some circumstances, an effective means of reducing frustrations, or at least of reducing the connection between frustration and political disaffection. But many other forms of political organization might accomplish this result, such as benevolent autocracy or charismatic dictatorship. If democracy is to make good its title as the only morally legitimate form of politics, then it must solve the problem of the heteronomous minority.

APPENDIX: THE IRRATIONALITY OF MAJORITY RULE

Majority rule can be called into question on grounds of its failure to preserve the liberty of the minority, but it has commonly been thought to be at least a rational method of making decisions, supposing that the members of the community are willing to agree upon its adoption. In fact it turns out that majority rule is fatally flawed by an internal inconsistency which ought to disqualify it from consideration in any political community whatsoever.

Self-consistency is perhaps the simplest sort of rationality which is demanded of all men in their deliberations and actions. If a man prefers a first state of affairs or action to a second, and prefers the second in turn to a third, then in all consistency he ought to prefer the first to the third. There is of course no psychological law which forces a man to keep his preferences consistent, any more than to adopt only means which he believes are well suited to his ends. But in exploring the theoretical possibility of a legitimate state, we are surely justified in positing a community of citizens who rise to that first level of rationality.

Presumably, also, we desire that the method of group decision which we adopt will lead to collective action having the like virtue of internal consistency. Unanimous democracy achieves this end, for it reproduces in the laws of the state the common preferences of the entire citizenry. If their preferences are consistent, so too will be those of the state. It might be thought that majority rule also preserved consistency of preference, but the facts are otherwise. As a simple example will illustrate, it is perfectly possible for a group of rational individuals with consistent preferences to arrive, by majority rule, at a completely inconsistent order of group preference! Suppose for the sake of simplicity that the community consists of three individuals who are faced with the problem of establishing a social ranking among three alternatives.[12] Each member of the voting community is first asked to rank the three possibilities in order of his relative preference. He may use any criteria he chooses—such as social utility, personal interest, or even whim—but he must be consistent. The group then establishes its collective preference by voting for the alternatives, two at a time. Since there are three alternatives, which we can call A, B, and C, there will be three votes in all: first A against B, then A against C, and finally B against C.

The preference order of the society is completely determined by the preference orders of the individuals, for whenever a pair of alternatives is presented to them, each man consults his private ranking and votes for the higher of the two. Now, there are a great many possible sets of private orderings which, when amalgamated by the device of majority rule, will produce a consistent public ordering. For example, consider the set of orderings in Table 1.

Table 1.

Individual I	Individual II	Individual III
A	A	B
C	B	C
B	C	A

Since Individuals I and II prefer A to B, they outvote Individual III, and the society as a whole prefers A to B. Simi-

12. The paradox, or inconsistency, which is developed in the text may be duplicated in any case involving two or more voters and three or more alternatives, assuming that one is permitted to be indifferent between any pair of alternatives, as well as to prefer one to the other. The "voter's paradox," as it is called, has been known for some time, and was actually the subject of an extended treatise by the nineteenth-century mathematician Charles Dodgson, better known as Lewis Carroll.

larly, Individuals II and III outvote Individual I and commit the society to B over C. Now, if the society prefers A to B, and B to C, then in all consistency, it ought also to prefer A to C. And so indeed it does, for Individuals I and II vote that preference, and thereby overrule Individual III once more. In this case, majority rule has transformed a consistent set of individual or private preference rankings into an equally consistent social preference ranking. But unfortunately, it is not always so.

Consider the set of individual orderings of the same alternatives in Table 2.

Table 2.

Individual I	Individual II	Individual III
A	B	C
B	C	A
C	A	B

When we pair the alternatives and count the votes, we discover that there is a majority for A over B (Individuals I and II), and a majority for B over C (Individuals I and II), but *not* therefore a majority for A over C. Quite to the contrary, Individuals II and III prefer C to A, and therefore so does the society. The result is that the group as a whole, starting from perfectly consistent individual preferences, has arrived by majority rule at an absurdly inconsistent group preference.

It might be objected that we have presented a false picture of rule by the majority. Assemblies do not vote on all the pair-wise combinations of possibilities which are under consideration. They either vote for all at once, and allow a plurality to decide, or else they take measures up one at a time, adopting or rejecting them. It makes no difference. The contradictions which we have discovered in majority voting can be reproduced in any of the ordinary variations which might be adopted by an assembly. For example, suppose that the procedure is followed of voting on the alternatives one at a time, until one is adopted, which thereupon becomes law. Each citizen votes against a proposal if there is some alternative still in the running which he prefers. On the other hand, once a proposal has been voted down, it is eliminated from the contest and is ignored by the electorate. Under this system, one can easily show that the winning measure is determined (in the paradoxical case outlined above) solely by the order in which the possibilities are brought before the voters. To see that this is true, consider once more the pattern of preferences exhibited in Table 2. There are three alternatives, A, B, and C. Hence there are six different orders in which the alternatives can be presented to the assembly, namely ABC, ACB, BAC, BCA, CAB, and CBA. Let us see what happens in each case under the system of eliminative voting.

Case 1.   A is put before the assembly and loses, since two individuals prefer something else to it.

B is now put before the assembly and wins, for with A eliminated, there are now two individuals who prefer it to anything else (i.e., to C), and only one who still has a prior preference for C.

So B wins.

Case 2.   A is put before the assembly and loses; C is put before the assembly and also loses; leaving B, which wins.

Case 3. By the same line of reasoning, when B is put before the assembly it loses; whereupon A also loses,
leaving C, which wins.

Case 4. B loses; C wins.

Case 5. Starting with C, which loses, we end up with A,
which wins.

Case 6. A wins.

In short, when alternative A is voted on first, alternative
B wins; when alternative B is voted on first, alternative C
wins; and when alternative C is voted on first, alternative
A wins. It is clearly irrational for a society to change its
preference among three alternatives whenever it considers
them in a different order. That would be like saying that
I prefer chocolate ice cream to vanilla when I am offered
chocolate first, but prefer vanilla to chocolate when I am
offered vanilla first!

Kenneth Arrow, in an important monograph entitled
Social Choice and Individual Values, has demonstrated
that the inconsistency of the voter's paradox infects virtually every method of social choice which can lay a reasonable claim to being called "democratic." How can it
be that when rational men with consistent preferences
make collective decisions by the apparently legitimate device of majority rule, they may arrive at inconsistent group
preferences? What is it about the process of collective decision which introduces an element of irrationality?

The answer seems to be contained in a very interesting
discovery of Duncan Black concerning the conditions under which majority rule can be trusted to yield consistent

results. It is obvious that we can guarantee the consistency of majority rule if we are permitted to set limits to the patterns of individual preference which the voters may adopt. In the extreme case, for example, if we require everyone to adopt the *same* preference order, then of course majority rule will simply reproduce that order as the social preference, which will be consistent. But are there any *reasonable* restrictions that will do the job? And, further, what is the weakest restriction that will ensure a consistent social preference order? The answer to the latter question is not yet known, but Black has demonstrated that under one interesting and natural restriction, majority rule will work consistently.

Briefly, the restriction is that every individual's preference order must exhibit the characteristic which he calls "single-peakedness" when plotted on a single scale. This means that there is some one-dimensional array of all the alternatives, on which each individual can locate his first choice, and which has the property that for every individual, the farther to the right an alternative is from his first choice, the less he prefers it, and the farther to the left an alternative is from his first choice, the less he prefers it. We are all familiar with such an array, namely the "left-right" spectrum in politics. If we string out the various political positions on the spectrum from extreme left, or radical, to extreme right, or reactionary, then the following is true: First, each individual can locate himself along the spectrum; Second, once he has found his place, which is the position of his first choice, then the farther to the right or left something is, the less he likes it.[13] For ex-

13. But notice, nothing can be said about his relative preferences among one position to the right and another to the left. This is because the ordering of his preference is ordinal, not cardinal.

ample, a moderate Republican prefers a conservative to a radical, and he also prefers a liberal Republican to a moderate Democrat. A left-wing Democrat prefers a socialist to a Communist, and also a middle-of-the-road Democrat to an Eisenhower Republican. And so forth. Black has demonstrated mathematically that if every person can satisfactorily fit his preferences onto such a spectrum, then majority rule must give a consistent social preference.

It is not completely clear what the deeper significance is of Black's discovery. One clue seems to be that single-peakedness, or arrangement along a left-right spectrum, occurs when everyone in the society views the alternatives as embodying varying degrees of some one magnitude. This is roughly akin to Aristotle's notion of virtue as a mean between extremes. Each virtue is seen as occupying a position on a scale, midway (roughly) between an excess and a defect. For example, courage is analyzed as a mean between rashness and cowardice. Presumably, the further one errs toward the direction of either extreme, the worse one is. In politics, we might interpret the left-right spectrum as a reflection of varying degrees of government intervention in social questions. At one end are the conservatives, who desire minimum intervention; at the other end are the socialists, who desire maximum intervention; and strung out between the two are various types of moderates who favor a mixture of intervention and nonintervention.[14]

When a single individual evaluates alternatives, the vari-

14. Notice that in this case, the conservatives and socialists do not focus their attention upon the same variable, but rather on two different variables which may be supposed to vary together. The conservatives are concerned with intervention *per se*, but the socialists are presumably concerned with social welfare and social justice, which they believe varies directly with the degree of intervention.

able or variables with which he is concerned presumably remain the same throughout his evaluation. This is one of the sources of his internal consistency. But when many individuals evaluate the same objective alternatives, they may do so in terms of a diversity of variables. The result is that when their decisions are collectively amalgamated through voting, the group preference may embody the inconsistency of standards of evaluation which existed, in a disaggregated form, in the voting population. It would seem, therefore, that majority rule has the best chance of yielding consistent results when the entire citizenry views the issues as polarized, in terms of variables which make it natural to prefer alternatives less and less as they diverge, in either direction, from one's first choice.

In order to see how lack of single-peakedness can lead to inconsistency, let us take a look at a simplified society in which there are three voters, a conservative, a welfare-state liberal, and a socialist, who must choose among three alternatives, namely laissez-faire capitalism, welfare-state liberalism, and socialism. The conservative, we may assume, would prefer laissez faire first, welfare-state liberalism second, and socialism last. It is also plausible that the liberal would prefer welfare-state liberalism first, socialism second, and laissez-faire capitalism last. But the socialist, who locates himself at the extreme left of the political spectrum, and prefers socialism first, might *not* prefer the welfare state second. He might in fact think that the welfare state had the worst features of both laissez-faire capitalism and socialism, with the virtues of neither. The welfare state throttles individual initiative, which does after all have a number of socially desirable consequences under capitalism, while also laying upon the society the burden of bureaucracy devoid of the rational total control possible under socialism. The socialist's preference order might therefore read socialism first, laissez faire second, and the welfare state last. Table 3 summarizes these individual preference orders:

Table 3.

Conservative	Liberal	Socialist
laissez faire	welfare state	socialism
welfare state	socialism	laissez faire
socialism	laissez faire	welfare state

What would be the result of a vote? The society would prefer laissez faire to the welfare state, two-to-one; it would also prefer the welfare state to socialism, two-to-one. But it would *not* prefer laissez faire to socialism. Quite to the contrary, by a vote of 2 to 1 it would prefer socialism to laissez faire. Thus even when the members of a voting assembly see the alternatives as embodying varying degrees of a single magnitude (state control), there may still not be a single-peakedness, and hence no consistency in the group preference.

III.
Beyond the
Legitimate State

———— •◆• ————

1. The Quest for the Legitimate State

We have come to a dead end in our search for a viable form of political association which will harmonize the moral autonomy of the individual with the legitimate authority of the state. The one proposal which appears genuinely to resolve the conflict, namely unanimous direct democracy, is so restricted in its application that it offers no serious hope of ever being embodied in an actual state. Indeed, since it achieves its success only by ruling out precisely the conflicts of opinion which politics is designed to resolve, it may be viewed as the limiting case of a solution rather than as itself a true example of a legitimate state.

A contractual democracy is legitimate, to be sure, for it is founded upon the citizens' promise to obey its commands. Indeed, any state is legitimate which is founded upon such a promise. However, all such states achieve their legitimacy only by means of the citizens' forfeit of their autonomy, and hence are not solutions to the fundamental problem of political philosophy. Majoritarian democracy claims a deeper justification than merely an original promise. It presents itself as the only viable form of political community in which the citizenry rule themselves, and thus preserve their autonomy while collecting their individual authority into the authority of the state. Unfortunately, our examination of the various arguments in support of majority rule has revealed that this additional claim is unfounded. Whatever else may be said for a majoritarian democracy, it does not appear to be true that the minority remain free and self-ruled while submitting to the majority.

Our failure to discover a form of political association which could combine moral autonomy with legitimate authority is not a result of the imperfect rationality of men, nor of the passions and private interests which deflect men from the pursuit of justice and the general good. Many political philosophers have portrayed the state as a necessary evil forced upon men by their own inability to abide by the principles of morality, or as a tool of one class of men against the others in the never-ending struggle for personal advantage. Marx and Hobbes agree that in a community of men of good will, where the general good guided every citizen, the state would be unnecessary. They differ only in the degree of their hope that so happy a condition can ever be realized.

Nor does our dilemma grow out of the familiar limitations of intellect and knowledge which afflict all but the most extraordinary men. It may be that in a technologically complex world only a few men can hope to master

the major political issues well enough to have genuinely
personal convictions about them. By positing a society of
rational men of good will, however, we have eliminated
such well-known obstacles to the fully just state. The magnitude of our problem is indicated by our inability to solve
the dilemma of autonomy and authority even for a utopian
society! By and large, political philosophers have supposed that utopia was logically possible, however much
they may have doubted that it was even marginally probable. But the arguments of this essay suggest that the just
state must be consigned the category of the round square,
the married bachelor, and the unsensed sense-datum.

If autonomy and authority are genuinely incompatible,
only two courses are open to us. Either we must embrace
philosophical anarchism and treat *all* governments as non-
legitimate bodies whose commands must be judged and
evaluated in each instance before they are obeyed; or else,
we must give up as quixotic the pursuit of autonomy in the
political realm and submit ourselves (by an implicit promise) to whatever form of government appears most just
and beneficent at the moment. (I cannot resist repeating
yet again that if we take this course, *there is no universal
or a priori reason for binding ourselves to a democratic
government rather than to any other sort.* In some situations, it may be wiser to swear allegiance to a benevolent
and efficient dictatorship than to a democracy which im-
poses a tyrannical majority on a defenseless minority. *And
in those cases where we have sworn to obey the rule of the
majority, no additional binding force will exist beyond
what would be present had we promised our allegiance to
a king!*)

It is out of the question to give up the commitment to

moral autonomy. Men are no better than children if they not only accept the rule of others from force of necessity, but embrace it willingly and forfeit their duty unceasingly to weigh the merits of the actions which they perform. When I place myself in the hands of another, and permit him to determine the principles by which I shall guide my behavior, I repudiate the freedom and reason which give me dignity. I am then guilty of what Kant might have called the sin of willful heteronomy.

There would appear to be no alternative but to embrace the doctrine of anarchism and categorically deny *any* claim to legitimate authority by one man over another. Yet I confess myself unhappy with the conclusion that I must simply leave off the search for legitimate collective authority. Perhaps it might be worth saying something about the deeper philosophical reasons for this reluctance.

Man confronts a natural world which is irreducibly *other*, which stands over against him, independent of his will and indifferent to his desires. Only religious superstition or the folly of idealist metaphysics could encourage us to assume that nature will prove ultimately rational, or that the opposition between man and objects must in principle be surmountable. Man also confronts a social world which *appears* other, which *appears* to stand over against him, at least partially independent of his will and frequently capricious in its frustration of his desires. Is it also folly to suppose that this opposition can be overcome, and that man can so perfectly conquer society as to make it his tool rather than his master? To answer this question, we must determine whether the appearance of the objectivity of society is also reality, or whether perhaps here, in the realm of institutions and interpersonal relationships, man's estrangement from the society which dominates him is accidental, adventitious, and ultimately eradicable.

Each individual is born into a social world which is already organized into regular patterns of behavior and expectation. At first, he is aware only of the few persons in his immediate physical environment and of their qualities and appearance. Very soon, the infant learns to expect repeated sequences of behavior from those around him. Later still, the child comes to see these significant persons as playing certain defined roles (mother, father, teacher, policeman) which are also played by other persons in different situations (other children also have mothers and fathers, etc.). The learning of language reinforces this awareness, for built into the word "father" is the notion that there may be many fathers to many children. The child matures and develops a personality by identifying with various role-bearers in his world and internalizing as his own the patterns of behavior and belief which constitute the roles. He *becomes* someone in this way, and also *discovers* who he is by reflecting on the alternatives which life offers him. Characteristically, the adolescent goes through a period of role definition during which he tentatively tries on a variety of roles, in order to test their appropriateness for him. (This is perhaps a description biased by contemporary Western experience. In some cultures, of course, the uncertainty over roles which produces an "identity crisis" never occurs since it is laid down by the society what set of roles the individual shall internalize and act out. For the purposes of this discussion, however, that point is not significant.)

Thus, the social world presents to each individual an objective reality with independently existing structures, just as the physical world does. The infant learns where his body ends and the objects around him begin. He distinguishes between what is within his control (various movements of his body) and what does not respond to his will. In exactly the same way, he learns to recognize the intractable realities of his social environment. When a boy is asked what he wants to be, he is really being asked which already existing social role he wishes to adopt as an adult. His answer—that he wants to be a fireman, or an engineer, or an explorer—indicates that he understands perfectly well the nature of the question. He may see himself, at least in a society like ours, as exercising some control over the roles which he shall adopt; but neither the questioner nor the boy would suppose that either of them has any control over the existence and nature of the roles themselves! Even the social rebel characteristically opts for an existing role, that of bohemian, or beatnik, or revolutionary. Like all role-players, such rebels wear the clothes, live in the quarters, and use the language appropriate to the role which they have chosen.

In any reasonably complex society, social roles are in turn organized into even more extensive patterns of behavior and belief, to which we apply the term "institutions." The church, the state, the army, the market are all such systems of roles. The characteristic interactions of the constituent roles of an institution are determined independently of particular individuals, just as the roles themselves are. At this level of complexity of organization, however, a new phenomenon appears which vastly increases the apparent objectivity of social reality, namely what has come to be known as the "paradox of unintended consequences." Each person in an institutional structure pursues goals and follows patterns at least partially laid down for him by the society—that is, already existing when he takes on the role and hence *given* to him. In his roles, however, he should be able to see the relationship between what he does and what results, even though he may not feel free to alter his goals or try new means. In the process of interaction with other individual role-players, more far-reaching results will be produced which may be neither anticipated nor particularly desired by any person in the system. These unintended consequences will therefore appear to the role-players as somehow not their doing, and hence objective in just the way that natural occurrences are objective. To cite a classic example, as each entrepreneur strives to increase his profit by cutting his price slightly, hoping thereby to seize a larger portion of the total market, the market price of his commodity falls steadily and everyone experiences a decline in profits. If he thinks about it at all, the entrepreneur will characteristically suppose himself to be caught in the grip of a "falling market," which is to say a natural or objective force over which he has no control. Even after he recognizes the causal relationship between his individual act of price-cutting and the drop in the market price, he is liable to think himself powerless to reverse the workings of the "laws of the marketplace." (Perhaps it is worth noting that, contrary to the assumptions of classical liberal economic theory, the entrepreneur is as much in the grip of social forces when he plays the role of capitalist as when he feels the pinch of the market. Even the most casual cross-cultural comparison reveals that "economic man" is a social role peculiar to certain cultures, and not at all the natural man who emerges when the distorting forces of tradition and superstition are lifted.)

The experience of the entrepreneur is reduplicated endlessly, so that men come to imagine themselves more completely enslaved by society than they ever were by nature. Yet their conviction is fundamentally wrong, for while the natural world really does exist independently of man's beliefs or desires, and therefore exercises a constraint on his will which can at best be mitigated or combatted, the social world is nothing in itself, and consists merely of the totality of the habits, expectations, beliefs, and behavior patterns of all the individuals who live in it. To be sure, insofar as men are ignorant of the total structures of the institutions within which they play their several roles, they will be the victims of consequences unintended by anyone; and, of course, to the extent that men are set against one another by conflicting interests, those whose institutional roles give them advantages of power or knowledge in the social struggle will prevail over those who are relatively disadvantaged. But since each man's unfreedom is entirely a result either of ignorance or of a conflict of interests, it ought to be in principle possible for a society of rational men of good will to eliminate the domination of society and subdue it to their wills in a manner that is impossible in the case of nature.

Consider as an example the economic institutions of society. At first, men play their several economic roles (farmer, craftsman, trader, fisherman) in complete ignorance of the network of interactions which influence the success of their endeavors and guide them into sequences of decisions, for good or ill, whose structure and ultimate outcome they cannot see. These same men imagine themselves encapsulated in a set of unchanging economic roles whose patterns, rewards, and systematic relationships are quite independent of their wills. Slowly, as the systematic interconnections themselves become more complex and mutually dependent, man's understanding of the economy as a whole grows, so that, for example, entrepreneurs begin to realize that their profits depend upon the total quantity of goods produced by themselves and their fellow capitalists, and the accumulation of individual desires for those goods which, collectively, constitute the level of demand. The first stage in the mastery of the economy may consist simply in the discovery of such aggregate quantities as demand, supply, interest rate, profit level, and even market price. That is to say, men must *discover* that the interaction of many individual acts of buying and selling establishes a single market price, which reflects the relation of supply to demand of the commodity being marketed. After realizing that such a marketwide price exists, men can begin to understand how it is determined. Only then can they consider the possibility of making that price a direct object of decision, and thus finally free themselves from the tyranny of the market.

In addition to the ignorance which enslaves even those in positions of power in the economy (the capitalists in a laissez-faire system), the pursuit of private interest results in the exploitation and enslavement of those whose roles in the economy carry relatively little power. Hence even the farthest advance imaginable of social knowledge would not suffice to liberate all men from their social bonds unless it were accompanied by a transformation of private interest into a concern for the general good. But if so utopian a condition were achieved, then surely men could once and for all reconquer their common product, society, and at least within the human world, move from the realm of necessity into the realm of freedom. Death and taxes, it

is said, are the only certainties in this life; a folk maxim
which reflects the deep conviction that men cannot escape
the tyranny of either nature or society. Death will always
be with us, reminding us that we are creatures of nature.
But taxes, along with all the other instruments of social
action, are human products, and hence must in the end
submit to the collective will of a society of rational men
of good will.

It should now be clear why I am unwilling to accept as
final the negative results of our search for a political order
which harmonizes authority and autonomy. The state is a
social institution, and therefore no more than the totality
of the beliefs, expectations, habits, and interacting roles of
its members and subjects. When rational men, in full
knowledge of the proximate and distant consequences of
their actions, determine to set private interest aside and
pursue the general good, it *must* be possible for them to
create a form of association which accomplishes that end
without depriving some of them of their moral autonomy.
The state, in contrast to nature, cannot be ineradicably
other.

2. Utopian Glimpses of a World Without States

Through the exercise of *de facto* legitimate authority,
states achieve what Max Weber calls the imperative coordination of masses of men and women. To some extent,
of course, this coordination consists in the more-or-less
voluntary submission by large numbers of people to institutional arrangements which are directly contrary to their
interests. Threats of violence or economic sanction play a

central role in holding the people in line, although as Weber very persuasively argues, the myth of legitimacy is also an important instrument of domination.

But even if there were no exploitation or domination in society, it would still be in men's interest to achieve a very high level of social coordination, for reasons both of economic efficiency and of public order. At our present extremely advanced stage of division of labor, relatively minor disruptions of social coordination can produce a breakdown of the flow of goods and services necessary to sustain life.

Consequently, it is worth asking whether a society of men who have been persuaded of the truth of anarchism— a society in which no one claims legitimate authority or would believe such a claim if it were made—could through alternative methods achieve an adequate level of social coordination.

There are, so far as I can see, three general sorts of purposes, other than the domination and exploitation of one segment of society by another, for which men might wish to achieve a high order of social coordination. First, there is the collective pursuit of some *external* national goal such as national defense, territorial expansion, or economic imperialism. Second, there is the collective pursuit of some *internal* goal which requires the organization and coordination of the activities of large numbers of people, such as traffic safety, to cite a trivial example, or the reconstruction of our cities, to cite an example not so trivial. Finally, there is the maintenance of our industrial economy whose functional differentiation and integration—to use the sociologist's jargon—are advanced enough to sustain an adequately high level of production. Is there any way in

which these ends could be served other than by commands
enforced by coercion and by the myth of legitimacy?

I do not now have a complete and coherent answer to
this question, which is in a way the truest test of the political philosophy of anarchism, but I shall make a few suggestions which may open up fruitful avenues of investigation.

With regard to matters of national defense and foreign
adventure, it seems to me that there is much to be said for
the adoption of a system of voluntary compliance with governmental directives. If we assume a society of anarchists—
a society, that is to say, which has achieved a level of
moral and intellectual development at which superstitious
beliefs in legitimacy of authority have evaporated—then
the citizenry would be perfectly capable of choosing freely
whether to defend the nation and carry its purpose beyond
the national borders. The army itself could be run on the
basis of voluntary commitments and submission to orders.
To be sure, the day might arrive when there were not
enough volunteers to protect the freedom and security of
the society. But if that were the case, then it would clearly
be illegitimate to command the citizens to fight. Why
should a nation continue to exist if its populace does not
wish to defend it? One thinks here of the contrast between
the Yugoslav partisans or Israeli soldiers, on the one hand,
and the American forces in Vietnam on the other.

The idea of voluntary compliance with governmental
directives is hardly new, but it inevitably provokes the
shocked reaction that social chaos would result from any
such procedure. My own opinion is that superstition rather
than reason lies behind this reaction. I personally would
feel quite safe in an America whose soldiers were free to
choose when and for what they would fight.

Voluntary compliance would go far toward generating sufficient social coordination to permit collective pursuit of domestic goals as well. In addition, I believe that much could be done through the local, community-based development of a consensual or general will with regard to matters of collective rather than particular interest. In the concluding chapter of my book, *The Poverty of Liberalism*, I have offered a conceptual analysis of the several modes of community. I will simply add that achievement of the sorts of community I analyzed there would require a far-reaching decentralization of the American economy.

This last point brings me to the most difficult problem of all—namely, the maintenance of a level of social coordination sufficient for an advanced industrial economy. As Friedrich Hayek and a number of other classical liberal political economists have pointed out, the natural operation of the market is an extremely efficient way of coordinating human behavior on a large scale without coercion or appeal to authority. Nevertheless, reliance on the market is fundamentally irrational once men know how to control it in order to avoid its undesired consequences. The original laissez-faire liberals viewed the laws of the market as objective laws of a benevolent nature; modern laissez-faire liberals propose that we go on confusing nature and society, even though we have the knowledge to subordinate the market to our collective will and decision.

Only extreme economic decentralization could permit the sort of voluntary economic coordination consistent with the ideals of anarchism and affluence. At the present time, of course, such decentralization would produce economic chaos, but if we possessed a cheap, local source of power and an advanced technology of small-scale production, and if we were in addition willing to accept a high level of economic waste, we might be able to break the American economy down into regional and subregional units of manageable size. The exchanges between the units would be inefficient and costly—very large inventory levels, inelasticities of supply and demand, considerable waste, and so forth. But in return for this price, men would have increasing freedom to act autonomously. In effect, such a society would enable all men to be autonomous agents, whereas in our present society, the relatively few autonomous men are—as it were—parasitic upon the obedient, authority-respecting masses.

These remarks fall far short of a coherent projection of an anarchist society, but they may serve to make the ideal seem a bit less like a mere fantasy of utopian political philosophy.

A Reply to Reiman

Shortly after I published this essay, Jeffrey H. Reiman mounted a full-scale attack on its theses in an answering essay, *In Defense of Political Philosophy*. Harper & Row has graciously agreed to my proposal for a new edition of my book in which I reply to Reiman's critique, and I must now try to defend myself as best I can against his forceful onslaught. Usually, this sort of exchange is reserved for learned journals or the letters columns of journals of opinion, books being rather clumsy vehicles for genuine, as opposed to stage-managed, dialogues.

The reactions to my essay have been varied, as one might expect. Some critics have thought I was merely irrelevant, others that I was logically confused, and at least one has suggested that it was immoral of me to publish the book at all. Paul T. Menzel sums the situation up nicely in the opening paragraph of an essay designed to defend me, after a fashion, against my enemies:

If published reactions are any indication of the response of the philosophical community to a philosopher's argument, Robert Paul Wolff's *In Defense of Anarchism* has perhaps persuaded and impressed its readers as little as any recently published work.

After due reflection on the objections advanced by Reiman and the others, I have come to the conclusion that I was dead right, and that my position is even better than I originally thought. With the help of my critics, I think I am now in a position to state my thesis in a stronger form and to defend it more satisfactorily.

Reiman's Case

As I understand Reiman, his defense of political philosophy proceeds in four stages, most of which are completed in the first two chapters of his book. Since my analysis of his argument will at some points become rather detailed, it will help to have the whole argument before us in outline form before we proceed to a criticism of it. The steps are as follows:

1. The definition of "authority" which I offer is logically confused, a *contradictio in adjecto* as he puts it. Such "moral authority" is directly inconsistent with the conditions of being a moral agent in general. Hence, if my aim is to argue that no one ever has authority in *that* sense of the term, I could more than adequately have handled the subject in a paragraph.

2. But from the impossibility of *moral* authority, nothing follows for politics (or indeed, for anything else), be-

cause it is *political* authority that states claim and anarchists deny. Political authority is *the right to use coercion to compel compliance with commands.* States do indeed claim that sort of authority, and the task of political philosophy is, in the first instance, to determine the circumstances under which such claims are valid.

3. Broadly speaking, the criterion of legitimacy of political authority—that is to say, the standard for evaluating a state's claim to the right to compel compliance to its commands by coercion—is the goodness of the consequences of the totality of laws which constitute the political system. In evaluating a state's claim to legitimate *political* authority, we must compare the probable consequences of its system of laws with those of other systems which might reasonably be considered possible substitutes, as well as with the probable consequences of an absence of any system of laws at all.

4. When a state passes the test of legitimacy, its possession of political authority creates a *prima facie* obligation on the part of the citizen to obey the law. That obligation is not overriding, but it is also not negligible. There will be a convergence of legitimate laws and the citizen's duty, but not (as I suggested) an absolute identity. In some real life situations, the *prima facie* obligation to obey the law will be overridden by other, weightier obligations. Therefore, legitimate political authority is compatible with moral autonomy. Wolff is wrong; political philosophy lives.

Reiman has some other things to say about the inadequacies of my analysis, including the historical observation that anarchists care about coercion, not about mere moral autonomy. (He is partly right and partly wrong about this.)

But these four steps embody the heart of his refutation, and
if I am to sustain my position, I must deal with them directly. As we shall see, Reiman's argument turns on two
points: the definition of political authority, and the notion
of a *prima facie* obligation to obey the commands of a legitimate state. Now let us take a look at the argument step
by step.

Step One: The Incoherence of the Notion of Moral Authority

Reiman begins by arguing that I have posed a pseudo-
problem to which there neither could be nor need be a
solution. How can the moral autonomy of the individual,
I ask, be made compatible with the (moral) authority of
the state? It can't, Reiman answers, because the notion of
authority as the right to be obeyed is simply contradictory
to the notion of moral obligation itself. A "philosopher of
mathematics" might just as sensibly ask how one can make
a triangle out of two straight lines.

Now, Reiman and I agree completely on this point, so
why do we seem to be on opposite sides of the fence? I
suggest that we are actually in serious disagreement about
three other propositions, all of which are worth disputing.
First of all, Reiman thinks it is obvious that what he calls
moral authority is an incoherent notion. I agree that it is incoherent, but I don't think that fact is quite so obvious as he
imagines. During most of the two and one half millennia
that moral philosophy has been written in West, claims of
moral authority have found acceptance among respectable
thinkers. The Catholic Church in particular, and western
religion in general, have demanded obedience either to

God's commands or to the edicts of His church. Despite the presence of "protestant" strains in christian thought before the modern era, it is only in the past four hundred years that anything like a doctrine of moral autonomy has gained currency. Immanuel Kant is the great spokesman for the thesis that every single rational agent must decide for himself what is right, and the books in which he so persuasively argued that claim are not yet two hundred years old. Reiman acknowledges that states make the sort of authority claim I describe, but he isn't impressed by that fact. As he puts it:

> Let us not be deceived by the fact that all states attempt to engender in their subjects a *feeling* or *belief* that there is a duty to obey the law or the ruler simply because it is the law or he is the ruler. *The question is, is the moral duty to obey essential to the concept of political authority?* We shall argue that it is not. (p. 19)

This leads us to our second disagreement, which concerns the significance of classical democratic theory. I believe that social contract theory, with its central reliance upon a strict notion of the consent of the governed, is a direct attempt to overcome the conflict between the primary demand of moral agency, which is autonomy, and the primary demand of state authority, which is obedience. If the criterion of legitimacy is good effects, then what is the point of demanding that those who are ruled must consent to be ruled? Or—to put the point in its stricter and more correct form—that those who are commanded must, either in their own persons or through their representatives, be the authors of the commands? One might, of course, point out that men are more tractable when they imagine that they have had a role in the making of the laws, but that is merely an argument for social engineering, not for democracy. Reiman's failure to confront democratic theory's premise of popular sovereignty undermines his entire argument. Indeed, when he finally does speak of consent in Chapter Five, he contradicts everything he has said earlier in his analysis of political authority.

The third disagreement between Reiman and myself directly concerns this notion of *political authority*. Reiman is willing to treat the state's claim to obedience as a mere "attempt to engender . . . a feeling or belief" because he thinks the case for legitimate authority can be made on independent grounds. The legitimate state can be distinguished from the prepolitical state of nature without any invocation of a duty to obey, according to Reiman. I shall show that he is wrong.

Finally, Reiman disputes my treatment of the special case of unanimous direct democracy. I claimed that when the citizens of a state collectively make all the laws by unanimous vote, the autonomy of the individual is compatible with the authority of the state. Reiman says that this is nonsense. He is quite right. It may be that men are bound by the collective commitments they make, but such commitments do not create the sort of political authority I was attempting to analyse. I stand corrected.

Step Two: The Definition of Political Authority

In my definition of authority, I focused on the state's claim of a right to be obeyed. Reiman, instead, focuses on the means which the state claims to have a right to use in order to secure compliance. "Political authority," he says,

"is the right to make commands and use coercion to discourage noncompliance with them" (p. 18). Who is right,
Reiman or I?

In a sense, this is just a pointless dispute about words.
I want to use the word "authority" to mean "the right to
be obeyed." Reiman wants to use the word "authority" to
mean "the right to use coercion to secure compliance." Reiman agrees with me that no one ever has *authority* in my
sense of the word; and I agree with Reiman (as we shall
see) that men frequently have *authority* in his sense of the
word. So except for some clout that the word itself may
have acquired through long centuries of use and abuse, why
do we bother to argue? The answer will emerge, but it will
take a bit more discussion before it becomes clear.

First of all, let me grant a point and make a point. I
agree with Reiman that states claim the right to use coercion to compel compliance. But Reiman, in invoking Max
Weber's definition of authority (as I had also done), fails to
notice a most significant clause in that definition. Here are
Weber's words:

> A compulsory political association will be called a "state"
> if and in so far as its administrative staff successfully up-
> holds a claim to the *monopoly* of the *legitimate* use of
> physical force in the enforcement of its order.

A *monopoly*, Weber says. Just so. The state does not merely
claim the right to enforce its commands. It also claims that
no one else has such a right within its territory. In particular, it denies that its subjects have the right to use force to
compel compliance with any "commands" which they may
see fit to "issue." Now, this claim to a monopoly of legitimate or justified enforcement is absolutely central to the

traditional concept of the state, and Reiman's failure to take it into account completely undermines his analysis of political, as opposed to the prepolitical, condition. To see why this is so, we must do a bit of old-fashioned state-of-nature/civil society political philosophy.

In the absence of a legitimate political authority, men and women confront one another as moral agents *simpliciter*. Reiman and I agree with Locke that in such a prepolitical "state of nature," persons have moral obligations and rights, among which presumably are the obligation to respect the legitimate pursuits of others and the right of self-defense.[1] Each moral agent must decide for himself what he ought to do and that decision includes a choice of the means by which he shall do it. Although anyone in a state of nature is free to claim a monopoly of the legitimate use of force, no one can demonstrate such a claim in principle.[2]

Whether and when you think a man has the right to use force in the state of nature will depend on the moral principles you believe to be valid. A total pacifist might hold that no one in a state of nature has any right to use force against another person in pursuit of his ends, even in the extreme case of self-defense against an attack on his life. Those with different moral convictions might claim that one had the

1. Strictly speaking, I don't agree with Reiman about this now, although I did when I wrote *In Defense of Anarchism*. My present views are rather different, though I am not now able to articulate them clearly or defend them adequately. But this is a reply to the last book I wrote, not a preview of the next I hope to write, and since the disagreement between Reiman and myself does not turn on those deeper issues of moral philosophy, I have adopted the simplifying device of speaking from my earlier point of view.

2. I say "in principle" because in some special set of circumstances it might actually be true that one and only one person was morally right to use force to accomplish his ends. That mere contingency, however, would not give him adequate grounds for claiming a *monopoly* of the legitimate use of force.

right to use force in order to defend one's own life, or the
lives of one's family, or the life of any person under unwar-
ranted attack. Still others would hold that force may legiti-
mately be used in defense of one's possessions or style of
life. And some would assert that in a state of nature, each
man has the right to use force to accomplish whatever ends
he has set himself, even when such ends interfere with the
lives or possessions of others. It makes no difference for the
present dispute what particular views Reiman and I hold,
so long as neither of us is an absolute pacifist. I am not, and
the text of *In Defense of Political Philosophy* seems very
strongly to suggest that Reiman is not either. So we can take
it as agreed between us that in the prepolitical condition,
in the absence of a legitimate state, there are at least some
situations in which individuals have the moral right to use
force to accomplish their ends.

Now, the common theme of classical contractarian theory
is that men relinquish their natural right to self-protection
and the use of force when they collectively bring the com-
monwealth or republic or state into existence. Indeed, that
giving-up of the individual right to coercion is the defining
mark of the social contract. If men do not renounce the
private use of force, then no *public* body has been created
by the compact. There may be a meeting of the minds or a
community of interests or a substitution of negotiation for
the war of all against all, *but there is no state.* This point
seems too obvious to belabor, but since it goes to the heart
of Reiman's confusion, let us devote a page or so to some
passages from the familiar texts. First Locke:

> Man being born, as has been proved, with a title to per-
> fect freedom, and an uncontrolled enjoyment of all the

rights and privileges of the law of nature equally with any
other man or number of men in the world, hath by nature
a power not only to preserve his property—this is, his life,
liberty, and estate—against the injuries and attempts of
other men, but to judge of and punish the breaches of
that law in others as he is persuaded the offence deserves,
even with death itself, in crimes where the heinousness
of the fact in his opinion requires it. But because no political society can be nor subsist without having in itself
the power to preserve the property, and, in order there-
unto, punish the offences of all those of that society, there,
and there only, is political society, where every one of the
members hath quitted this natural power, resigned it up
into the hands of the community in all cases that exclude
him not from appealing for protection to the law established by it; and thus all private judgment of every particular member being excluded, the community comes to
be umpire; and by understanding indifferent rules and
men authorized by the community for their execution,
decides all the differences that may happen between any
members of that society concerning any matter of right,
and punishes those offences which any member hath committed against the society with such penalties as the law
has established; whereby it is easy to discern who are and
who are not in political society together. Those who are
united into one body, and have a common established law
and judicature to appeal to, with authority to decide con-
troversies between them and punish offenders, are in civil
society one with another; but those who have no such
common appeal—I mean on earth—are still in the state
of nature, each being, where there is no other judge for
himself and executioner, which is, as I have before shown
it, the perfect state of nature. (*Second Treatise Concerning Civil Government*, chapter 7)

Note particularly the last sentence. Those who are thus united "are in civil society one with another." Those who have not forfeited their right to be each "judge for himself and executioner" are "still in the state of nature."

Now Rousseau. Rousseau takes it for granted that the formation of civil society involves each man's forfeiture of the right to use his force at his own discretion. The real problem for political philosophy, as Rousseau sees it, is how to ensure that each member of the body politic, while thus alienating his natural liberty in order to gain a measure of security, shall nevertheless "obey only himself and remain as free as before." The solution, he claims, lies in the terms of the social contract:

> Each of us places in common his person and all his power under the supreme direction of the general will; and as one body we all receive each member as an indivisible part of the whole. (*The Social Contract*, book 1, chapter 6)

The effect of the social contract is to destroy the moral symmetry of the state of nature. Such a symmetry is anarchic just in the original sense that there is no *rule*, no party possessing rights of decision and enforcement which are not possessed by all. Whether a morally symmetrical society is orderly or chaotic depends on other factors which are not relevant to my dispute with Reiman. What is crucial is that civil society differs from the state of nature in exhibiting an asymmetrical distribution of rights and duties. Specifically, the state—whoever that may be—has the right to command and (in Reiman's interpretation) to use force to compel compliance, whereas individual citizens have an obligation to obey (my interpretation) or at least to refrain from using force to compel compliance to their particular wishes. To put the point in quasi-economic terms which capture something of the logic of traditional liberal political theory: by means of the social contract, a moral monopoly is substituted for the moral free market of the state of nature.

But Reiman *rejects* the monopolistic claims of the traditional theory! He agrees that citizens may, under special circumstances, be morally justified in resisting, defying, or evading the coercive efforts of even a just state. So it would appear that the dispute between us has dissolved. Not so, for in place of the claim to *monopoly*, Reiman offers a modest claim to what might be called *prima facie* monopoly. According to Reiman, "legitimacy [of the state] suggests *prima facie* reasons for obedience [by the citizen], which can be overridden by other moral considerations" (p. 35). But this watered-down claim has the same logical force as the traditional claim of absolute monopoly, for the classical distinction between a state of nature and civil society rests *not* on the *absoluteness* of each citizen's renunciation of private force, but only on his renunciation *in some degree* or *to some extent* of the right to use force. If the renunciation is absolute, then the state does indeed acquire a *monopoly* of the legitimate (i.e., rightful) use of force. And Reiman to the contrary notwithstanding, states everywhere and always claim such a monopoly. If, on the other hand, the renunciation is only partial, then the state acquires a *prima facie* right to the employment of force over and above the right which each individual had and to some extent still retains. In either case, the perfectly symmetrical moral situation of the state of nature, in which each person has the same rights and duties vis-à-vis each other, is exchanged for an asymmetrical moral relationship in which one party, the state, has a preponderant right to force vis-à-vis all the others. To put the point somewhat differently, a citizen will need better reasons to justify his defiance of a legitimate state than the state will need (aside from appeals to its legitimacy *per se*) to justify its coercion of him, for the state's appeal to its legitimacy *per se* will count as a reason of some weight all by itself.

In my original essay, I took the traditional theory as my target. Reiman thinks he can turn aside my attack on legitimacy by claiming for the legitimate state no more than a *prima facie* right to coercion which is not shared by each citizen. But as I shall show, his argument fails to establish even such a *prima facie* right. The truth is that there is no legitimate political authority either in the classical sense of a monopoly of the use of force compatible with the autonomy of the individual or in Reiman's sense of a *prima facie* right to the use of force possessed by the state but not by the individual. I need hardly add that for the purposes of this dispute between myself and Reiman, it makes not the slightest difference how large or small a weight one assigns to that supposed *prima facie* right. My position is that one must assign zero weight to it, and Reiman's position is that one must assign some nonzero weight to it. If I can refute even so modest a claim for the Legitimate State, then I will have considerably strengthened my original thesis.

Let us return to Reiman's definition of political authority as "the right to make commands and use coercion to discourage noncompliance with them." So far as making commands is concerned, of course, that is something anyone can do. As Hotspur says, after Glendower has boasted that

he can call spirits from the vasty deep, "Why, so can I, or
so can any man;/ But will they come when you do call for
them?" So the essence of political authority, in Reiman's
view, is the right to use coercion to enforce one's wishes.[3]
Whoever has that right can be said to have political authority.

But this commits Reiman to a very peculiar conclusion
indeed. By his definition, in a state of nature every single
person has actual or potential political authority over every
other person. Assuming, as I have, that Reiman is not an
absolute pacifist, suppose that I return home one night in a
state of nature (so to speak) to find a burglar breaking into
my house. I command him to get away from my house immediately, not, however, adding a threat to call the police
since in a state of nature there are no police. Now if Reiman
will agree that I have the moral right to use some measure
of force to "discourage [the burglar's] noncompliance"
with my command, then he thinks that I have "political
authority" over the burglar! What is more, if Reiman also
thinks that the burglar has the moral right to use force to
defend himself against an attack by me that goes beyond
what is required to drive him away from my house, then to
that degree the burglar has "political authority" over me
(if he has the foresight to "command" me to stop trying to
kill him before he resorts to force in self-defense).

Something has obviously gone wrong here. Reiman and I
were engaged in a serious debate about the grounds and

3. Lest it seem that I am somehow sliding around Reiman's definition by speaking of enforcing wishes rather than commands, let me
say that Reiman's argument rests in part on the institutional or systematic character of law, as opposed to the noninstitutional character
of the actions and decisions of private individuals. I shall deal with
that part of his theory of political authority a bit later on, when I turn
to his criterion of the legitimacy of political theory.

limits of legitimate political authority, and all of a sudden I am drawing facetious conclusions about the political authority of burglars and householders. Reiman doesn't mean to impute political authority to every private individual who has a moral right to use force on some occasion or other. Indeed, he isn't concerned with individuals at all when he defines political authority. Reiman is talking about the putative political authority of *states*. It is the commands of the *state* which are to be complied with or not; it is the *state* which claims to have the right to use coercion to discourage noncompliance; *states* are said to have, or not to have, political authority. Individuals may have rights against the state; they may be morally justified in defying the state; they may even be right to deny entirely some actual state's claim to political authority. But individuals do not have, or claim, political authority—states do.

And now we have come to the very center of Reiman's confusion. Like so many defenders of the state who have gone before him, Reiman suffers from what we may diagnose as a virulent case of *mystification*. By mystification I mean the tendency to use language so as to conceal the real nature of a thing, in particular to conceal the real moral or power relations among persons, their real interests, and the real status of their rights and obligations. Reiman's talk about the state thoroughly obscures its real nature. He encourages us to reify the state, to conceive it as having an ontological status different from that of individual persons, to blind ourselves to the real locus of moral responsibility in political relationships, and thereby to construe the relationship between the individual and the state in an entirely false way.

On the very first page of my essay, I define the state as "a group of persons who have and exercise supreme authority within a given territory." The state is *a group of persons*. It is not an institution, if by that is meant something other than the people who occupy the roles which constitute that institution. It is not a system of laws, if by that is meant something other than the persons who make, interpret, and enforce the laws. The state is a group of persons. Reiman says that he accepts this statement (p. 19), but over and over again his use of language obscures its force. Consider, for example, the following passage from the Introduction:

> To put it somewhat crudely, what Wolff fails to see is that the proposition "Everyone *should* determine his own moral duty" (Wolff's anarchism) in no way implies the proposition "Everyone *should* be allowed to do what he determines as his moral duty" (political anarchism). (p. xxiii)

We are invited to contrast my anarchism with political anarchism by comparing parallel propositions. But Reiman, by slipping into the passive voice in the second proposition ("should be allowed"), destroys the parallelism and obscures the most important question, namely, who does the allowing? He fosters in the reader the illusion that there is a contrast between the subjective judgments of the individual citizen and the objective dictate of a state which is somehow more than merely other persons. The impersonality of that phrase, "should be allowed," changes the subjective, fallible, autonomous moral judgment of the judge or policeman or legislator into the voice of the law, of "society," of the STATE. Here are some other passages, scattered through Reiman's essay, which exhibit the same reification and exaltation of the state:

[P]olitical systems *begin* from the *assumption* that some areas of behavior are too crucial to the mutual well-being and survival of the community to be left to the consciences of its members. (p. 29)

Political systems start from the assumption that some forms of behavior must be prevented, even if they are conscientiously chosen. *This is the logic of political systems.* (p. 29)

The political or legal system . . . of the state can be expressed as the principles specifying when and in what form force will be applied to coerce behavior into or out of certain forms. (pp. 21–22)

In these passages, and in many others like them, a sort of conceptual conjuring trick has been performed. It is clear enough who is to be the object of the force and coercion: it is the citizen, the individual whose behavior is to be altered. But the other party to the coercive interaction has somehow vanished into thin air. Rather like the Cheshire Cat, nothing is left but the state, smiling benevolently and impersonally (or perhaps malevolently, but still always impersonally).

The real fact, of course, is that when a citizen is coerced, some other real flesh and blood person does the coercing, in the active voice. Not "force will be applied" but "Jones, who is a policeman or a judge or a prison guard, will apply force to Smith, who is a citizen." The state is either a real group of persons or it is a fiction.

If we can hold the real nature of the state firmly in mind, we will recognize that Reiman's theory of political authority had failed to do the job for which it was intended. It does not distinguish between the relations among men in a prepolitical state of nature and the relations among them in civil or political society. Either all moral agents have the right, under some conditions or other, to use force to implement their purposes, or else none do. In the absence of a collective agreement to forfeit that right—an agreement, I have argued, which would carry with it a forfeiture of autonomy—men remain in a moral state of nature, regardless of the beliefs that some or all may have about the supposed special right to force of that small group who call themselves the state.

Step Three: The Criterion of Legitimacy

I think Reiman would actually agree with the major thesis of this argument, although he might take exception to my manner of expressing it, because I have so far omitted a factor on which he places very great weight. The confrontation between the individual and state is not, Reiman insists, merely a confrontation between a small group of people (the individual) and a large group of people (the state). Rather, it is a confrontation between an individual and a *system of laws*. A page or so ago I quoted three statements from Reiman, and in the third I omitted a parenthetical aside. Here is the passage again, with the parentheses restored:

The political or legal system (and the two are used here interchangeably, in that it is the legal system which makes the political system a "system," i.e., a rule-governed totality as opposed to a simple fact of domination)

*of the state can be expressed as the principles specifying
when and in what form force will be applied to coerce behavior into or out of certain forms.* (pp. 21–22)

If "the state" were merely a group of individuals deploying
force to compel compliance, then we would have "a simple
fact of domination," which Reiman would evaluate morally,
I imagine, in much the same way as I. But a state is a political system, a system of rules. Good or bad, "it must be
judged as only a system of general principles can be judged,
in terms of their general foreseeable effects" (p. 32). The
individual, on the other hand, is *not* a system of rules, nor
do his decisions, insofar as he acts as a private citizen, constitute such a system of rules. To be sure, real individual
people occupy the positions defined by the system of laws,
and in their roles as judges, legislators, prosecutors, or defense attorneys, make the decisions and take the actions by
which the system of laws is implemented. But when they
deliberate about the morally right thing to do, their reasoning takes one of two quite different forms. When considering a particular application of the laws, or even the legitimacy of a particular law within the total system of law,
their concern is (or at least ought to be) for procedural
justice and constitutionality. That is to say, they seek to
ensure that persons are treated equally before the law,
that relevantly similar cases are treated in a similar manner, and that the procedures for the adoption and application of laws have been adhered to. When they evaluate the
legitimacy of the entire system of laws, on the other hand—
an evaluation which they must, as autonomous moral agents,
continuously be involved in making—then their concern is

for the moral value of the totality of expectable results of
the system as a whole. In Reiman's words, the legitimacy of
a political system is determined by answering the question:

> Will [it] tend to yield more morally worthy results than
> can be expected from the absence of a political system,
> or more morally worthy results than—or at least as much
> as—can be expected from other possible and viable polit-
> ical systems? (p. 32)

In short, Reiman espouses a version of what might be
called rule-consequentialism rather than act-consequential-
ism when it comes to evaluating a political system. But he
does not claim that the subjects of a rule-consequentially
legitimate state have an *absolute* or *over-riding* obligation
to obey the laws of the state, even when the total foreseeable consequences arc the best that are realistically possible.
Rather, he claims only that they have a *prima facie* obligation to obey such a state, conditional upon their evaluation
of the other and possibly conflicting *prima facie* obligations
that their situation may also lay on them.

Step Four: The *Prima Facie* Obligation
to Obey the Law

We finally have Reiman's answer to the central question
between himself and me: "Wherein does our moral situation as subjects of a legitimate state differ from our moral
situation in a state of nature?" The classical democratic
answer is, In a state of nature each of us is morally autonomous and each has the right to use force to compel compliance with what he judges to be his morally justified

commands; but in a legitimate state, no private citizen has any right to use force for such a purpose—only the state has. My answer is, In a state of nature each of us is morally autonomous and each has the right to use force to compel compliance with what he judges to be his morally justified commands; a special authority can be acquired by some group of persons called "the state" only at the price of the moral autonomy of the subjects, and that is a price that it is contrary to the nature of rational agents to pay. Reiman's answer is, In a state of nature each of us is morally autonomous and each has the right to use force to compel compliance with what he judges to be his morally justified commands (Reiman doesn't put it this way, but I think he would grant the claim); but under a system of laws which is rule-consequentially maximal, each subject has a new *prima facie* duty to obey the laws, over and above whatever obligations (and rights) he had in the state of nature. As Reiman says, in a legitimate state, the subject's legal obligation is "simply one morally relevant factor figuring in his determination of his moral obligation" (p. 38).

Reiman offers no demonstration of this claim, despite its centrality to his position.[4] Now I do not in general approve of the philosophical tactic of playing the idiot, of claiming not to understand some statement that looks perfectly comprehensible on the face of it. But I must confess that I genuinely do not understand the usual appeals to *prima facie* obligations. In the writings of W. D. Ross, where it plays a central role, the notion is based upon a theory of

4. In the discussion of *prima facie* obligation which follows, I am drawing on and in part reproducing remarks which I made in a reply to two other critics, Professors Malcolm B. E. Smith and Michael S. Pritchard. See *The Journal of Value Inquiry* (Winter 1973) for the entire exchange.

a power of moral intuition which I find opaque and impossible either to explicate or to translate into some other, more comprehensible terms. We are supposed by Ross simply to know further how much weight their rightness is to be given in a deliberation among conflicting *prima facie* duties. The intuitionist position, even in the careful and intelligent version offered by Ross, seems to me simply no position at all—rather like Leibniz's pre-established harmony or a religious man's appeal to faith.

Sometimes, however, the notion of *prima facie* obligation is introduced as part of a "rational reconstruction" of our ordinary moral consciousness. That is to say, it is claimed that our moral reasoning actually makes appeal to such a notion, and that the deliberations of serious and intelligent moral agents can be construed to involve appeal to the notion of conflicting *prima facie* duties, whether or not anything quite that precise and explicit is actually expressed.

I reject the use of the notion of *prima facie* obligation as construed in this manner because in the end a rational reconstruction of moral consciousness is a description of men's moral convictions rather than a justification of them, and it is a justification that I seek. I readily grant that many mature, serious, reflective students of politics believe that we have a *prima facie* obligation to obey the valid laws of a constitutional democracy. I deny this belief. I have never heard any plausible argument for it, and it seems to me merely a superstitious submission to authority.

It might be thought that I am being unduly harsh with Reiman and inaccurate to boot, for he makes no appeal to an inexplicable power of moral intuition. He explains quite clearly what the grounds are for the imputation to the citizen of a *prima facie* duty of obedience, namely, the goodness of the general foreseeable results of the operation of the legal system *as a system.* Where is the mystery in that?

The answer is a bit tricky, but it is essential to the dispute between Reiman and myself, for the notion of a *prima facie* rather than an overriding duty of obedience is the last refuge of the myth of state authority. Once we have exposed the emptiness of even this diminished claim, there will be no further justification to be offered for the state's pretensions. Reiman and the other defenders of the state will have to acknowledge that autonomous moral agents are always in a state of nature vis-à-vis one another. Only an autonomy-sacrificing contract can alter their moral relationship.

Reiman's invocation of a *prima facie* duty of obedience involves a sort of double counting which is entirely unjustified and which has the practical effect of tilting the scales in favor of the *de facto* state in any dispute between it and an individual. To see how this double counting comes about, let us develop an example in some detail.

Suppose that a friend comes to me and asks me to back up a lie he has told to Internal Revenue agents who are investigating his tax returns. He has claimed a number of business deductions for lunches and dinners at which he says that he and I discussed plans for a joint publishing venture. The deduction has been challenged, and he wants me to sign an affadavit swearing that I did eat with him on those occasions and that we did discuss business. All of this, let us further suppose, is quite false. Now I must engage in a moral deliberation, weighing a number of considerations which may count as reasons for and against complying with his request.

Just what I consider to be relevant considerations, and what weight I give, positive or negative, to each will depend on the particular moral theory or set of moral opinions which I hold. For example, I may take into account that he is a good friend, that on past occasions he has gone out of his way to help me when I was in need, that I am a husband and father with responsibilities to my family which may be compromised if I am caught out in the lie (a fact which I will properly discount by the degree of probability that I will be caught), and that the amount of money involved is so small as to make only a marginal difference to my friend. I will also take into account the purposes for which the government is likely to use the tax money it collects. I will weigh my evaluation of the tax structure in general, including its fairness or unfairness in distributing tax burdens among the citizens of this country. I will add into my calculation some estimate of the probable effects of my lie on the future law-obedience of myself, my friend, and any others who may learn of it (possibly giving positive weight to a negative effect if I believe that there is too high a level of obedience to law in myself and my friend, or a negative weight if I believe he and I are insufficiently law-abiding). I may also assign some negative weight to lying in and of itself.

At some point in my moral deliberations (which the reader may think have already gone on quite long enough), I will attempt to judge the constitutionality of the tax laws under which my friend is being investigated, and I will extend my examination of the subject so far as to consider the effect on the total system of laws of my proposed violation. If I judge the system of laws to be generally felicific in its consequences, then I shall discount their value as an actually operating system of laws by my estimate of the degree of effect which my violation will have upon them, and add that discounted weight on whichever side of the balance is appropriate. I might conclude, for example, that the legal system of the United States is highly beneficial, but that it would be even better if there were somewhat more defiance on the part of individual citizens. (I might believe, for instance, that obedience to law is, in the Aristotelian sense, a virtue, the excess of which is slavish servility and the defect of which is anarchic self-indulgence.) I might also judge that my defiance was likely to have very little effect one way or the other on the law-obedience of either myself, my friend, or my fellow-citizens. Nevertheless, all this (and more, of course) will go into my calculation.

Now, up to this point, no question of legitimacy of state authority has been raised. The several weights and their balance will presumably vary from state to state and from case to case, but the *sorts* of considerations relevant to the deliberation will be exactly the same in a monarchy, a popular dictatorship, a constitutional democracy, and a military autocracy. Some of the factors are particular, in the sense that they relate to the individual case alone. Such, in this instance, are my indebtedness to my friend for past favors, my own personal obligations, and so forth. Other factors, such as my estimate of the beneficence of the system of laws as a whole, are more general, and might enter in virtually the same way into many different calculations (although the details of each case may alter the weights to be assigned even to general factors by altering the probabilities of outcomes—one act of law-defiance might carry virtually no likelihood of influencing the behavior of others, while a second might reasonably be predicted to affect the behavior of thousands or even millions of other citizens).

In a state of nature, when this point had been reached, the deliberation would be at an end. Assuming that some way could be found to quantify the various "weights," a sum would be struck and the decision taken either to co-operate with my friend's lie or not. But according to Rei-man, in certain political communities one more "morally relevant" factor must be added into the calculation before it is complete. If the system of laws as a whole is what I have for the sake of brevity called consequentially maximal, then that fact will create a new additional *prima facie* obligation of obedience to the law, and I am morally bound to add its weight to that of the other arguments against complying with my friend's request.

And here, I contend, we see the precise nature of Rei-man's confused double counting. Some philosophers use the notion of a *prima facie* obligation merely as a short-hand way of summarizing the aggregate weights of those factors which I have called "general." To say that there is a *prima facie* obligation to obey the laws of a generally beneficent state is for them just a compendious way of reporting that the general factors weigh out on the side of compliance, allowing of course for shifts in probabilities from case to case. Since the general factors remain relatively constant over a span of time in which many particular decisions must be made, this reminder to myself in the form of a *prima facie* obligation claim will shorten my calculations. Presumably, I would then stand under a general necessity of periodically reviewing my estimate of this portions of my deliberations, revising and altering it as changes in the facts, the system of laws, and the solidity of predictions of the future required.

If this summary sense of a *prima facie* duty is all that

Reiman has in mind, then he has no right to add in a *new* weight for the *prima facie* duty after he has already added in the weights of the individual general factors. *Either* he must simply add the *prima facie* obligation to the estimate of the particular factors, or else he must carry out the entire calculation of both particular and general factors. To carry out the entire calculation and then add the *prima facie* duty is to count the weight of the general factors twice. But if Reiman thinks that there is more to *prima facie* duties than a mere summary of the aggregate weight of certain sorts of factors, then he has said absolutely nothing to justify such a belief. Indeed, his general adoption of consequentialism in moral deliberations should rule out any appeals to emergent or supervenient *prima facie* duties.

The net effect of Reiman's mistake is to load the scales in favor of compliance with the law. It is easy to see this in the imaginary case we have been considering. The violation of tax laws by two private citizens will, in most cases, have so little effect on the general operation of the legal system and the social level of law-obedience that an honest calculation of effects will assign a vanishingly small weight to this factor even when one judges the system as a whole to be highly beneficial. A *prima facie* obligation, unquantified but vaguely felt to be of some significance, is likely to be assigned a considerably greater weight. Hence, individuals who are misled by Reiman into confusing the summary and supervenient sense of *prima facie* obligation are likely to conclude for obedience in many cases where a straightforward consequentialist calculation would lead to disobedience.

Leaving to one side such estimates of actual deliberative

outcomes, however, we arrive at the clear theoretical conclusion that the notion of a *prima facie* obligation to obey
the laws of a consequentially maximal state offers no way
of distinguishing the moral condition of the state of nature
from that of civil society. Even in the state which Reiman
chooses to call *legitimate,* an individual will carry out exactly the same moral calculation that he would perform in
a state of nature (or, what is presumably the same thing,
in an illegitimate state). No new morally relevant consideration will be introduced into the calculation in the
legitimate state. Which means, of course, that in any ordinary sense of the word, the state is *not* "legitimate." In
short, I am not wrong. Political philosophy, as the study of
that legitimate political authority which distinguishes civil
society from the state of nature, is dead.

Beyond Reiman

Thus far, I have confined myself to the particular attack
which Reiman mounts against my thesis. but other critics
might not wish to limit themselves to his line of reasoning.
I have argued that only a contract could bring into existence
a new moral situation, but could I not resolve the conflict
that I perceive between authority and autonomy by putting
the notion of *prima facie* obligation to my own uses? In my
original essay, I made much of the totality of the forfeiture
of autonomy which the classical social contract demands of
each individual. Suppose that a watered-down contract
were proposed, calling only for such forfeiture as was involved in granting to the state a *prima facie* right to command and laying upon the citizen only a *prima facie* obli-

gation to obey. Does not such a contract leave room for autonomy?[5]

My answer is, of course, no. But before explaining why, I want once again to emphasize the absoluteness of the typical state claim to authority. In the United States, for example, the law permits what is called conscientious objection in cases involving religious or quasi-religious scruples. But the state claims the right to decide what shall be accepted as a conscientious objection, and in which contexts the appeal to conscience shall be allowed. The law also permits private citizens to use force in self-defense, but the state claims the right to decide when force may be used, against whom, for what purposes, and within what limits. The state claims the right to change its decisions on these matters at any time, so long only as it does so in accordance with its own rules. No state anywhere, to my knowledge, relinquishes in the slightest its claim to be the supreme authority within its territory. If it were to relinguish that claim even so little as to make room for the most marginal exercise of authority by private citizens, then when the state and some citizen came into conflict within that margin, the two together would have to resolve their differences either as equals through force or negotiation or else by submission of the dispute to a higher authority. In the first case they would be back in a state of nature and in the second the state would thereby have acknowledged that it was not sovereign.

5. It is clear, I hope, that Reiman takes no such line. For him, the validity of the *prima facie* obligation rests on the goodness of the systematic effects of the laws. For even this sort of diminished contractualist position, the validity of the *prima facie* obligation rests on the bindingness of the original contract.

Let us consider, then, a social contract calling only for a transfer to the state of *prima facie* rather than overriding authority. Wherein lies the forfeiture of autonomy in such a contract? In my original essay, I pointed out that autonomy could be forfeited totally or by degrees, across the board or with regard only to particular areas of decision, and so forth. Obviously a contract of the sort we are now considering would involve a diminished forfeiture of autonomy, and I suppose it would therefore be preferable to a total forfeiture of autonomy. But the signatories of this contract would still have bound themselves to obey commands whose rationale they either denied or could not comprehend. To revert to the example of my friend and his tax troubles, I would be bound under such a contract to refuse to help him, even though the outcome of my calculation of pros and cons was a clear conclusion to comply with his request. To produce that result, it would only be necessary that the net weight in favor of lying for him be less than the standing weight of my *prima facie* obligation to obey the law. Since the good consequences of law-obedience would already have been added into my calculation, I would be reduced to saying, "I shall obey the law solely because it is the law, irrespective of any reasons I can give myself concerning the goodness or badness of the law and the goodness or badness of my complying with it in this case." That is heteronomous obedience just as surely as is the absolute obedience to state commands demanded by classical social contracts.

The belief in state authority comes naturally to men, it would appear. A band of robbers ride into town with guns drawn and demand all the gold in the bank. They are called criminals. They return the next year on the same day and repeat their demand. Again they are called criminals. They put on uniforms and return each year on the same day. Eventually, they are called tax collectors. Finally, the smallest and least offensive of the bandits rides into town unarmed and the townspeople give him their gold without a struggle. The state has arrived.

Index